LORD, WHERE ARE YOU

WHEN BAD THINGS HAPPEN?

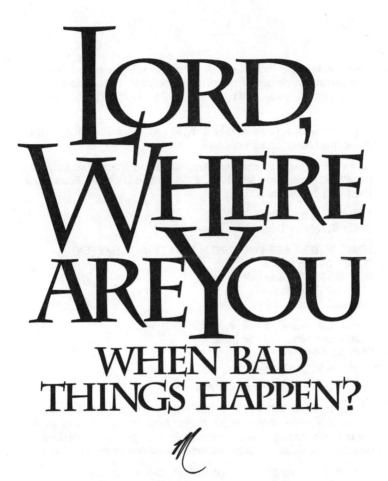

LORD, WHERE ARE YOU WHEN BAD THINGS HAPPEN?

KAY ARTHUR

Edited by Larry Libby
Cover design by Durand Demlow

LORD, WHERE ARE YOU WHEN BAD THINGS HAPPEN?
© 1992 by Kay Arthur
Published by Multnomah Press
10209 SE Division Street
Portland, Oregon 97266

Multnomah Press is a ministry of
Multnomah School of the Bible
8435 NE Glisan Street
Portland, Oregon 97220

Printed in the United States of America.

Library of Congress Cataloging-in-Publication Data
Arthur, Kay, 1933-
    Lord, where are you when bad things happen? / Kay Arthur.
        p.   cm.
    ISBN 0-88070-529-9
        1. Bible. O.T. Habakkuk—Criticism, interpretation, etc.
2. Theodicy. I. Title.
BS1635.2.A78 1992
224'.9506—dc20   92-16177
                                                                        CIP

93 94 95 96 97 98 99 00 01 - 10 9 8 7 6

CONTENTS

HOW TO USE
THIS BOOK

God, where are you when bad things happen? It's a question people asked in Habbakkuk's time and it's a question that is still asked today. You, dear student, picked up this book because this question lingers in your heart. You wonder, *If God is God, why doesn't He do something about the evil and injustice in the world?*

Be encouraged! This book will involve you in a daily study of God's Word which will help you see for yourself God's answers to these tough questions. It's an investment of time over a ten-week period which will reap incredible dividends. Be diligent in your study and you will learn much.

This book is ideal for personal devotions, home Bible studies, and Sunday school material. You don't need any helps to do the study, but the following are available and may enhance what you learn: supplementary teaching tapes on video and audio for adults and teens—one for each chapter in the book. These can be rented or purchased. There are also leader's tapes and a manual to help you in your discussion. For more information on these helps, please write:

Precept Ministries
P.O. Box 182212
Chattanooga, TN 37422
(615) 892-6814

Before you begin your study, ask God to open your eyes and heart so you can accurately discern His truth.

Kay

Chapter 1

HE'S THERE, LISTENING TO THE CRY OF YOUR HEART

DAY ONE

Has there ever been a time when you questioned God?

Possibly you found yourself in a trial you never *dreamed* would happen to you. Maybe you cried for help, and it seemed God didn't hear. You weren't delivered. You suffered.

When you watch the evening news or pick up the newspaper, do you wonder, *Where is God? If He is God and in charge of this universe, why does He allow the world to continue on its course of self-destruction? Why doesn't He put an end to all the cruel and bizarre things happening in our society?*

Do you know about something that has happened to a child of God that seemed so unjust, so evil that you doubted God? In the secret chambers of your mind, have you wondered how God could allow such things to happen to those who belong to Him? Maybe you wouldn't allow yourself to verbalize such a question because it would seem unholy. But have you wondered, *Where is God when bad things happen?*

A friend of mine was raped. She had heard me tell stories of others in similar situations who had called on God and were delivered. So in the darkness of fear she, too, cried out to God. In a trembling voice she commanded the man to stop in the name of Jesus. He didn't. Why didn't God answer her cry and deliver her?

Where was God?

A twenty-year-old girl, a personal friend of ours, a Christian with a sterling reputation, was found brutally murdered in her bedroom.

Where was God?

Hitler exterminated God's chosen people—men, women, and children—in gas chambers and ovens.

Where was God?

In Communist countries countless Christians suffered for their faith, living on almost nothing, enduring the ravages of malnutrition, beatings, and hard labor. Others were committed to psychiatric institutions and subjected to all sorts of chemical treatments simply because they refused to be silent about their faith in Christ.

Where was God? *psalm. 24. 1-1*

The earth is The Lords. and all its Contains the World and those who Dwell in it

These are tough questions, aren't they? Skeptics delight in asking these questions. They are questions many of us would prefer to ignore . . . or bury under weak and insufficient theological theories.

Where is God when bad things happen?

It's a question that many who call Him Father want to avoid. It doesn't fit with their concept of God. They can't explain it from the Word.

Are we afraid to ask these questions for fear God will not have an answer? Or do we fear that if we find the answer, it will distort our view of God or make Him into someone we cannot explain or understand?

There are some who would have you believe that God, Who is a God of love, mercy, and compassion, does not have a thing to do with the evil that takes place in this world. But if He doesn't . . . then what does that imply about His power, His authority, His involvement in the affairs of men?

Are these new questions which, until now, have never troubled the heart of man? Oh, no, my friend! They are as old as human history. They are the questions of Habakkuk the prophet:

How long, O LORD, will I call for help,
And Thou wilt not hear?
I cry out to Thee, "Violence!"
Yet Thou dost not save.
Why dost Thou make me see iniquity,
And cause me to look on wickedness?..
Why dost Thou look with favor
On those who deal treacherously?
Why art Thou silent when the wicked swallow up
Those more righteous than they?
(Habakkuk 1:2-3a,13b).

These questions are the burden of Habakkuk's heart. He bears them without shame or apology. And rather than ignoring them, God has preserved these questions for all to read. His answer to Habakkuk is also His answer to us.

What a study lies in store for us! Your faith will grow immensely as you learn God's answers to these tough questions. It is my prayer that as you diligently study, you will learn how to walk with hinds' feet on high places through life's valleys.

Victory will come in the measure to which you give yourself to this study. You can skip questions, not write out the assignments, and do nothing but read what I have written. Yet I sincerely believe the benefits of this penetrating look into the heart of this neglected book of Scripture will be much greater and longer lasting if you participate wholeheartedly!

All of this study is designed with a purpose in mind. I urge you to shut yourself up each day in a quiet place where you can be still and know that He is God—where you can take His yoke upon you and learn of Him. Remember, grace and peace are multiplied to you through the knowledge of God and of Jesus our Lord (2 Peter 1:2).

What questions about God have you hidden in your heart? Write them out below; then, we will see how God will answer in the weeks to come.

Psalm 119-73 - Thy hands made me and
119—18 fashioned me. and give me
119—125 understanding that I may learn
119—169 thy commandments.
1 Cor - 2 - 12-13
2 Cor 3-5
2 Tim - 3-23
Why does terrible things happen to
Godly people

DAY TWO

We live in a world that is going the wrong way.

Men have forgotten God.

There is no fear of God before their eyes. In pride and arrogance they walk their own way, flaunting their sin, taking His name in vain. They refuse to blush, and demean those who do. They scorn anything which would restrain them from pursuing their desires. They are their own god!

Where is God? Why does He allow such things? Why do the wicked continue? Why do the wicked prosper? Why do the righteous suffer? Why aren't the righteous delivered? Why doesn't God hear the prayers of His people?

This was the cry, the dilemma of Habakkuk. And it is from Habakkuk's conversation with God that we will begin to find God's answers to our own dilemmas.

Therefore, Beloved, you need to stop and read through the book of Habakkuk. It's only three chapters long. You will find the New American Standard Version of Habakkuk printed in the back of this book.

Before you begin reading, ask the Holy Spirit to guide you into the truth. We cannot understand and discern spiritual truths apart from His work in our lives. Just as Paul prayed for the believers in Ephesians 1:17, we, too, need to ask the Lord to give us a spirit of wisdom and of revelation in the true knowledge of Him. We can be confident that He will answer because we have asked according to His will (1 John 5:14-15). Psalm 119:18 says, "Open my eyes, that I may behold wonderful things from Thy Law." Pause a few moments to confess to the Lord your inability to hear and discern truth apart from His enabling. Ask Him to enlighten the eyes of your heart so that you may truly know what He longs to show you. Thank Him that He will.

As you read Habakkuk, I'd like you to do several things:

1. The book of Habakkuk is a conversation between the prophet and his God. As you read through the text, note carefully *who* is speaking and *when* he speaks. Note when the conversation shifts from Habakkuk to God, and then back to Habakkuk. You might want to write this in pencil in the left-hand margin of the text in the back of this book. When you are finished and are sure you know when God is speaking and when Habakkuk is speaking, ink it in.

2. As you read, also note every question Habakkuk asks God. You might want to highlight these questions and, in the left-hand margin of the text, number each one.

3. How does the book of Habakkuk begin and end? Note the contrasts or similarities, depending on what you see.

Begain asking God where was he when he needs help? Distressed Confused Ends with praise and confidence

4. Does Habakkuk's situation change at the end of the book? How do you know?

He would rejoice in God who saved him, gives strength. positive attitude

5. What can you learn from what you have seen so far in the book of Habakkuk?

Although you may be tempted to skip this assignment because it will take a little while, *please don't*. As a teacher called of God, I long to help you know Him in a more intimate way so that you might live in the confidence of a strong, established faith. But that will not happen apart from spending time in the Word, for "faith comes from hearing, and hearing by the word of Christ" (Romans 10:17).

If you'll do as I ask, you will begin to get a glimpse of where God is when bad things happen.

DAY THREE

Have you ever thought of what it would be like to lose your freedom to some foreign power—especially a foreign power which was not sympathetic to your faith in Christ?

Habakkuk was distressed because the southern kingdom of Judah was threatened by a fierce and impetuous people called the Chaldeans, or Babylonians. Oh, the Babylonians might root and snort like a bull ready to charge, but in the minds of the Jews the Babylonians would *never* rule over them.

But then, isn't this typical? People rarely think something like that will happen to the country in which they live. The Israelites didn't think it could happen in Jerusalem. After all, they were God's elect nation. Jerusalem was the home of Solomon's magnificent temple. Besides . . . who could be closer to the sovereign God of all the earth than *Israel?*

To appreciate the book of Habakkuk and how it parallels our day, we must consider its historical context. That's the thrust of our study for the next two weeks.

You can gain a comprehensive and accurate understanding of any book of the Bible by becoming thoroughly familiar with the book itself.

1. Read through Habakkuk again, doing two things:

a. Look for every reference to the Chaldeans (Babylonians). Record all that you learn about them from the book of Habakkuk.

b. As you read, make a simple outline of Habakkuk by noting generally what is done in each chapter by either Habakkuk or God. Record your outline below.

Chapter One:

Habakkuk, ask about God telling the evil and wickedness to continue, & letting to allow a nation to over them

Chapter Two:

God answers them to write it down, Babylone by hurting other people they would be punished

Chapter Three:

God is going to disipline Judah by use the Babylone. ask God to give him strength to face it

2. Would the Chaldeans ever invade and conquer Judah? How do you know from the book of Habakkuk?

3. What about your country? Do you think it could ever happen where you live? What would you do?

DAY FOUR

Understanding Habakkuk's historical setting is vital—especially if you are unfamiliar with Israel's history. It will certainly help you in reading the Old Testament. And there is so much from the Old Testament we can apply to our own lives! First Corinthians 10:11, in reference to Israel, says, "Now these things happened to them as an example, and they were written for *our* instruction, upon whom the ends of the ages have come" (emphasis added).

After the death of Solomon, the nation of Israel was split into two kingdoms: the northern kingdom and the southern kingdom. The northern kingdom was composed of ten tribes and was called Israel. Israel went into idolatry immediately after it split from the other two tribes. In 722 B.C., it fell to the Assyrians.

The southern kingdom was composed of the tribes of Judah and Benjamin. It is often referred to simply as Judah. Its capital was Jerusalem.

At the time Habakkuk was written, the northern kingdom had already gone into captivity.[1] Habakkuk prophesied sometime between 621 B.C. and 609 B.C., which was before the Babylonian captivity. The Babylonian captivity of the southern kingdom, which

17

was on the horizon of Habakkuk's time, started in 605
B.C. when Nebuchadnezzar attacked Jerusalem and
took a handful of nobles and princes to Babylon.
Daniel was in that group. Then in 597 B.C. when King
Jehoiachin rebelled, Nebuchadnezzar again besieged
Jerusalem and took ten thousand captive. Among that
group was Ezekiel. The final siege and destruction of
Jerusalem happened in 586 B.C., when the city and the
temple were destroyed.

Nineveh, where Jonah prophesied, fell to the
Babylonians about 612 B.C., just as Nahum had fore-
told. By this time the Assyrians, who had captured the
northern kingdom of Israel, faded from view as a dom-
inant world power.

If you will take a few minutes to study the following chart from the *International Inductive Study Bible*,
it will help you put in perspective all I've said.

Habakkuk, a contemporary of the prophet Jeremiah,
probably lived during the time of King Josiah and,
therefore, experienced the revival which occurred
under Josiah. Jeremiah 1:1-3 tells us that Jeremiah
prophesied to the Kingdom of Judah during Josiah's
reign right through the exile of the southern kingdom in
586 B.C. This is the exile Habakkuk referred to when he
wrote, "I must wait quietly for the day of distress"
(Habakkuk 3:16).

Now, Beloved, in the light of all that history, take a
few minutes to read 2 Kings 22. It's a wonderful chapter. After reading it today, you will appreciate it so
much more when we discuss it tomorrow.

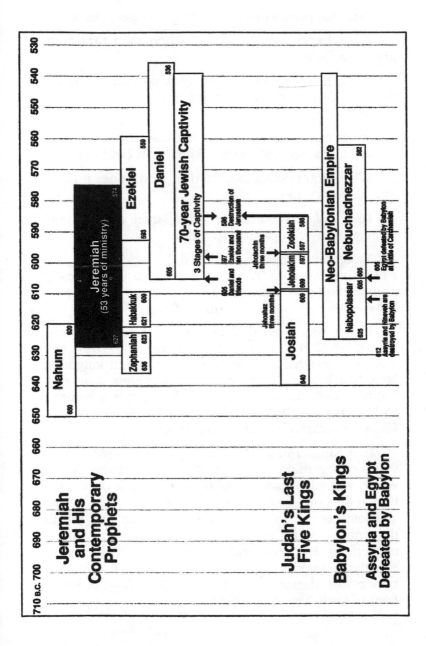

DAY FIVE

What happens when God's people neglect His Word?

What happens in a nation when men turn from knowing God?

What happens in the life of a church when the Word of God loses center stage and is given a minor or "bit" part?

What happens *to you* when day after day you neglect to spend time alone with God in His Word?

When you neglect the Word of God, does it make any difference in your life?

Let's look at what happened in Israel, and then see if there is any comparison to today.

Yesterday I asked you to read 2 Kings 22. Did you? I hope so. If not, do so now. It will give you a greater appreciation and understanding of what will follow in today's study.

Josiah was a good king. Second Kings 22 opens around 622 B.C. One hundred years earlier, the Assyrians invaded and captured the northern kingdom. Now Josiah became king when he was eight years old. Yet this was no surprise to God. Nothing is a surprise to Him because He is the sovereign, omniscient (all-knowing) ruler of the entire universe.

In 1 Kings 13:1-2, we read a prophecy given about 930 B.C. regarding the birth of Josiah and the events which will take place in his lifetime. This is over three hundred years before Josiah appeared in history. How awesome is our God! He calls into being that which does not yet exist. He moves in the affairs of mankind to perform His will, and brings His desires to pass exactly as they are predicted. Why do we refuse to bow before Him and honor Him as God, King of kings, Lord of lords, very God of gods?

20

Second Kings 22 focuses on the events that occurred in the eighteenth year of Josiah's reign when he was twenty-six years old. This makes the time about 622 B.C. Remember, Judah went into captivity in 586 B.C., thirty-six years later.

When Shaphan the scribe was sent to clean and repair the damages in the temple of God, Hilkiah the high priest, in the process of helping with these temple repairs, found a copy of God's Word. *Can you imagine?* The Word of God was lost in the house of God! What effect did this have on God's people?

Read 2 Kings 23:1-27, and you will see how religious people lived when they worshiped God without the knowledge of His Word. List the kinds of things in which they were involved.

They fell into idolatry, worshiping Baal and Asherah (2 Kings 23:4). They were also caught up in astrology (2 Kings 23:4-5), which was strictly forbidden by God in Deuteronomy 17:2-7. How this must have hurt our God!

Before I began writing today's lesson, I was on my face before our Father telling Him that I wanted to feed His sheep only His Word. May we find it, live by it, and not bring grief to the heart of our Lord.

21

DAY SIX

What happens in a nation when the Word of God is lost in the house of God? How does it affect the character of a nation?

Wherever you find idolatry, you will find immorality or some sort of sexual perversion. One follows on the heels of the other. Second Kings 23:7 tells us that male cult prostitutes were in the house of the Lord. They were part of the sexual immorality and perversion associated with Baal and Asherah worship.

This departure from the Word of God not only affected the morals of the people, it also endangered the lives of the children. In 2 Kings 23:10 parents made their children "pass through the fire for Molech." Is it any different today as our nation offers the blood sacrifices of aborted children on the altars of immorality? Just as they heard the screams of their children as the fire blackened their delicate skin, today can you not hear the screams and see the twisted writhing of the children's tiny bodies as their limbs are severed or as the flesh is burned from their bodies by the caustic saline injection used to abort babies?

But human sacrifice was not the only perversion. "God's people" had become involved in the occult. Although this association was expressly forbidden in Leviticus and Deuteronomy, the people turned to mediums and spiritists instead of consulting God. Behind idols, mediums, spiritists, and astrology, you will find demons (1 Corinthians 10:19-20).

Look around you.. Is it any different today? No! But has it always been this way in the United States of America? No; in your lifetime you have seen great changes in what is now condoned in America. Abortion used to be considered murder, and any doctor found performing an abortion was sentenced as a lawbreaker. Today, it is a common means of birth control. Even many churches will not take a stand against abortion.

At one time homosexuality and lesbianism were against the law, but now the law promotes their "rights." Some in the church call homosexuality nothing more than a "genetic predisposition." Others have established homosexual congregations, saying God is against promiscuity, but not homosexuality or lesbianism. They maintain it is merely an alternate lifestyle.

At one time even divorce was not tolerated in many denominations. Now some in the church divorce one another, then show up in church the next week with another spouse, and nothing is said. Church members are not held accountable for their behavior. For the most part, church discipline as set forth in 1 Corinthians 5 is no longer practiced.

Why are we in such a state? I believe it is because we've lost the Word of God—both in the house of God and in seminaries. Many graduate from seminary with thorough training in the technicalities of ministry and in psychology, but *they do not know how to study the Word and pray.*

Think about it. What place, what priority does the Word of God have in the lives of the majority of pastors, let alone churchgoers? Has your church lost the Word of God? Have *you* lost it?

What happened in Judah can happen again. It's the inevitable result of losing the Word of God. Over and over again, church history testifies to the effects of neglecting the Word. The church has been turned around only when a reformer has discovered, studied, lived by, and proclaimed the truths of God's Word in the hearing of His people.

Ask God to search your heart and to show you if you have neglected the Word of God. Be honest and open before Him as you ask Him to show you what, if anything, has taken priority over His Word. Ask Him what you need to do. Or, if you have given His Word its rightful place, spend time in worship and thanksgiving.

23

Renew your commitment, so that in all things He will have the preeminence. Record your commitment below.

DAY SEVEN

Anguish struck Josiah's heart when Shaphan the scribe read aloud the Book of the law that had been lost in the house of the Lord. King Josiah saw how far they had strayed from God's standard of holiness. Once Josiah heard God's Word, he understood the righteous wrath of God that had to be executed in holy judgment.

If God's Word has been lost in many churches, how can we even expect the world to be aware of the righteous commandments in the Word? So many write to tell me what has happened since they've started studying God's Word, learning it precept upon precept. As they've learned to dig out truth for themselves, their eyes have been opened to subtle errors which had crept into their thinking.

They see how they've been deluded by men's persuasive arguments, philosophies, and traditions.

They realize how they've bought into human reasonings and trendy teachings.

They discern how, in recent years, psychology and

self-preoccupation have replaced the Word and the cross.

They find themselves able to quote and expound the latest Christian bestsellers, but not the Word of God.

They acknowledge that without the plumbline of God's Word, they could not perceive how far out of alignment they were from truth.

Thinking they were in touch with themselves, they realize they have been out of touch with God and His truth. They see how they have been deceived, and how they have reaped the consequences of that deceit. And all because the Word of God had lost its proper place in their lives.

Take a few minutes and prayerfully read the following words from Colossians 2. Mark every "in Him" and "with Him" and list what the Colossians are to do in respect to Jesus Christ. Also, list Paul's concerns for the Colossians in this chapter. What had deluded them? Where were they out of line with truth? What were Paul's warnings? Be specific.

5 *in Him*   **COLOSSIANS 2:1-23**   *with Him 2*

For I want to know how great a struggle I have on your behalf, and for those who are at Laodicea, and for all those who have not personally seen my face, that their hearts may be encouraged, having been knit together in love, and attaining to all the wealth that comes from the full assurance of understanding, resulting in a true knowledge of God's mystery, that is, Christ Himself, in whom are hidden all the treasures of wisdom and knowledge. I say this in order that no one may delude you with persuasive argument. For even though I am absent in body, nevertheless I am with you in spirit, rejoicing to see your good discipline and the stability of your faith in Christ.

25

As you therefore have received Christ Jesus the Lord, so walk in Him, having been firmly rooted and now being built up in Him and established in your faith, just as you were instructed, and overflowing with gratitude.

See to it that no one takes you captive through philosophy and empty deception, according to the tradition of men, according to the elementary principles of the world, rather than according to Christ. For in Him all the fulness of Deity dwells in bodily form, and in Him you have been made complete, and He is the head over all rule and authority; and in Him you were also circumcised with a circumcision made without hands, in the removal of the body of the flesh by the circumcision of Christ; having been buried with Him in baptism, in which you were also raised up with Him through faith in the working of God, who raised Him from the dead. And when you were dead in your transgressions and the uncircumcision of your flesh, He made you alive together with Him, having forgiven us all our transgressions, having canceled out the certificate of debt consisting of decrees against us and which was hostile to us; and He has taken it out of the way, having nailed it to the cross. When He had disarmed the rulers and authorities, He made a public display of them, having triumphed over them through Him.

Therefore let no one act as your judge in regard to food or drink or in respect to a festival or a new moon or a Sabbath day—things which are a mere shadow of what is to come; but the substance belongs to Christ. Let no one keep defrauding you of your prize by delighting in self-abasement and the worship of the angels, taking his stand on visions he has seen, inflated

without cause by his fleshly mind, and not
holding fast to the head, from whom the entire
body, being supplied and held together by the
joints and ligaments, grows with a growth
which is from God.

If you have died with Christ to the elementary
principles of the world, why, as if you were living in the world, do you submit yourself to
decrees, such as, "Do not handle, do not taste,
do not touch!" (which all refer to things des-
tined to perish with the using)—in accordance
with the commandments and teachings of men?
These are matters which have, to be sure, the
appearance of wisdom in self-made religion
and self-abasement and severe treatment of the
body, but are of no value against fleshly indulgence.

Now read Paul's prayer for the Colossians in 1:9-12.
Personalize these truths by praying the verses back to
the Lord. Pray for yourself and for those whom the
Lord lays on your heart. You might want to write out
your prayer in the space below.

I cannot bring you to this point in our study without telling you what I believe can be a viable solution. Many are told to study God's Word, but are not told *how*, nor given the tools to do so. There is a tool which I believe can be revolutionary, one which will help you discover for yourself the teachings of every book of the Bible. It's the *International Inductive Study Bible*.[2] This study Bible is unique. In other study Bibles, what you study are the notes, conclusions, and observations of *others*. This Bible will show *you* how to discover the content of each individual book of the Bible, make your own study notes, and open the way for you to apply the truths you encounter to your life. It can be used by children and adults. Those who do so will never lose the Word of God again, for it will be at home in the temple of God (1 Corinthians 6:19). His Word will dwell in you richly (Colossians 3:16).

Notes

1. In the appendix of the *International Inductive Study Bible*, see the chart entitled "Israel's Division and Captivity."

2. You can call your Christian bookstore to order the *International Inductive Study Bible*, published by Multnomah Press. Or, write Precept Ministries, P.O. Box 182218, Chattanooga, Tennessee 37422, or call (615) 892-6814.

Chapter 2

HE'S THERE,
ADMIT YOUR SIN
AND EMBRACE HIM

DAY ONE

Many of you reading these words know what it is to live apart from the Word of God. So do I. If we live apart from the Word of God, our lives bear the scars of sin, for sin is transgression of the law (1 John 3:4).

The entire southern kingdom of Judah was scarred by sin—scarred because they had lost the Word of God. "Go, inquire of the LORD for me and the people and all Judah concerning the words of this book that has been found, for great is the wrath of the LORD that burns against us, because our fathers have not listened to the words of this book, to do according to all that is written concerning us," said King Josiah in 2 Kings 22:13.

What do you do when you suddenly see sin for what it is—when you suddenly become aware of a holy God who has every right to judge sin in His holy wrath?

Josiah's heart was tender to God's Word (2 Kings 22:19). He tore his clothes, humbled himself before God, and wept. No excuses, no covering up, no rationalizing, no blaming his sin or the sins of his people on another. Josiah owned Judah's sin; he took responsibility for it. Because of this, God heard Josiah's prayer and stayed His hand of judgment.

> "Because your heart was tender and you humbled yourself before the LORD when you heard what I spoke against this place and against its inhabitants that they should become a desolation and a curse, and you have torn your clothes and wept before Me, I truly have heard you," declares the LORD. "Therefore, behold, I will gather you to your fathers, and you shall be gathered to your grave in peace, neither shall your eyes see all the evil which I will bring on this place" (2 Kings 22:19-20).

Hearing the Word of God brought a godly sorrow that led to repentance. "And before him there was no king like him who turned to the LORD with all his heart and with all his soul and with all his might, according to all the law of Moses; nor did any like him arise after him" (2 Kings 23:25).

What about you? When you sin, are you sorry? With what kind of sorrow? Read the following passage from 2 Corinthians, marking every reference to sorrow in one way and every reference to repentance in another way so you can distinguish between the two. Then list below the text what you learn about the two kinds of sorrow.

2 CORINTHIANS 7:8-11

For though I caused you sorrow by my letter, I do not regret it; though I did regret it—for I see that that letter caused you sorrow, though only for a while—I now rejoice, not that you were made sorrowful, but that you were made sorrowful to the point of repentance; for you were made sorrowful according to the will of God, in order that you might not suffer loss in anything through us. For the sorrow that is according to the will of God produces a repentance without regret, leading to salvation; but the sorrow of the world produces death. For behold what earnestness this very thing, this godly sorrow, has produced in you: what vindication of yourselves, what indignation, what fear, what longing, what zeal, what avenging of wrong! In everything you demonstrated yourselves to be innocent in the matter.

Oh, my friend, maybe your sin has been very great. But if you will do as Josiah did, if you will humble yourself before God and in godly sorrow turn from lawlessness to submission to God's Word, if you will turn to God with all your heart, soul, and might, God will meet you just as He met Josiah. The wrath of God will fall on the ungodly of this world, but it will not touch you. Whether wrath comes as in Habakkuk's day or whether people repent and revival comes as it did in Josiah's day, you can rejoice in the God of your salvation . . . if you will but trust in God's Word.

God honored Josiah's obedience. However, the hearts of the people did not change. According to God, they had committed two evils. Listen to His words: "They have forsaken Me, the fountain of living waters," and they hewed "for themselves cisterns, broken cisterns, that can hold no water" (Jeremiah 2:13). God was to be their wellspring, the One to Whom they turned for satisfaction, help, and guidance. They were to be dependent upon Him. To live in total dependence upon Him would be to worship Him as He should be worshiped. Instead, they turned again to other sources.

In Jeremiah 2:18-19 God asked them, "But now what are you doing on the road to Egypt, to drink the waters of the Nile? Or what are you doing on the road to Assyria, to drink the waters of the Euphrates? Your own wickedness will correct you, and your apostasies will reprove you; know therefore and see that it is evil and bitter for you to forsake the LORD your God, and the dread of Me is not in you."

I see Egypt as a picture of the world. The Israelites were the slaves of Egypt, under the dominion of Satan. Similarly, until we come to know Jesus Christ personally, we are slaves of the world under the dominion of Satan, the prince of this world. Jesus is our Passover lamb, the one whose blood was shed to deliver us from sin and death (see 1 Corinthians 5:7, Hebrews 2:14). Once the children of Israel were delivered by the Lord from the "land of Egypt, from the house of bondage" through the blood of the Passover lamb, they were told to never return to Egypt. "Woe to those who go down to Egypt for help" (Isaiah 31:1).

God was their God. He would lead them, provide for them, protect them. They need not turn to the arm of flesh. Yet, here they were in the days of Jeremiah and Habakkuk, running to drink the waters of the Nile and the Euphrates when they had access to the Fountain of Living Waters! That's an Old Testament parallel to you and me walking in the flesh instead of walking in the Spirit.

Water, imperative for life, has always been a picture of God. Remember what happened during the Feast of Tabernacles?

> Now on the last day, the great day of the feast, Jesus stood and cried out, saying, "If any man is thirsty, let him come to Me and drink. He who believes in Me, as the Scripture said, 'From his innermost being shall flow rivers of living water'" (John 7:37-38).

In the Old Testament, God shows us that He alone is to be our life, our source, our sufficiency. Here in the New Testament, Jesus says the same thing. "Come" and "drink" are in the present tense in the Greek, which implies continual or habitual action. You and I are to live in total dependence upon God.

Now then, Beloved, you need to apply what you are learning. Are you depending upon God, running to Him? If not, where are you turning? Are you turning to a person, to a position, to material possessions—what you drive, what you wear, where you live—to give you a sense of worth, value, purpose, acceptance, satisfaction? At what fountain are you drinking to quench your thirst? Has it really satisfied? Write out your answer and the reason for what you say.

Depend upon God.
learned to depend upon God
more.

ESEGUIRE

So that you'll remember to live in total dependence on God, memorize John 7:37-38 and Philippians 4:19.

In the last day of the feast, Jesus stood and cried out saying, if any man thirsty, let him come to me and drink

He who believes in me as The scripture said from his innermost being shall flow rivers of living water

and my God shall supply all your needs according to his riches in glory in Christ Jesus

DAY THREE

When we love something or someone else more than we love God—whether it be a husband, wife, child, friend, profession, pleasure, or intellectual pursuit—God calls it harlotry.

When God redeemed His people from Egypt, He told them exactly how they were to live. He set before them ten major commandments, along with many rules and regulations for day-by-day living. The first commandment was to love Him above all else, "for I, the LORD your God, am a jealous God, visiting the iniquity of the fathers on the children, on the third and the fourth generations of those who hate Me, but showing lovingkindness to thousands, to those who love Me and keep My commandments" (Exodus 20:5-6).

To fail to love God above all else is to play the harlot with other lovers. This is why God said what He did to Jeremiah:

JEREMIAH 3:6-14

Then the LORD said to me in the days of Josiah the king, "Have you seen what faithless Israel did? She went up on every high hill and under every green tree, and she was a harlot there. And I thought, 'After she has done all these things, she will return to Me'; but she did not return, and her treacherous sister Judah saw it. And I saw that for all the adulteries of faithless Israel, I had sent her away and given her a writ of divorce, yet her treacherous sister Judah did not fear; but she went and was a harlot also. And it came about because of the lightness of her harlotry, that she polluted the land and committed adultery with stones and trees. And yet in spite of all this her treacherous sister Judah did not return to Me with all her heart, but rather in deception," declares the LORD.

And the LORD said to me, "Faithless Israel has proved herself more righteous than treacherous Judah. Go, and proclaim these words toward the north and say,

'Return, faithless Israel,' declares the LORD;
'I will not look upon you in anger.
For I am gracious,' declares the LORD;
'I will not be angry forever.
Only acknowledge your iniquity,
That you have transgressed against the LORD your God
And have scattered your favors to the strangers under every green tree,
And you have not obeyed My voice,' declares the LORD.
'Return, O faithless sons,' declares the LORD;
'For I am a master to you,
And I will take you one from a city and two from a family,
And I will bring you to Zion.'"

1. Go back and read this segment of Scripture once more. This time mark the following words in a distinctive way or in a specific color so that you can spot them immediately:

a. harlot, faithless, adultery, or adulteries
b. return
c. obeyed

2. What do you learn about the people even in the days of Josiah?

Have you played the harlot with God? Do you think, my friend, you can get away with it? You can't. Return to God with all of your heart, soul, mind, body, and strength.

DAY FOUR

" 'Judah did not return to Me with all her heart, but rather in deception,' declares the LORD" (Jeremiah 3:10).

Did you notice this verse in yesterday's lesson? You would think the southern kingdom of Judah would have learned a lesson when the northern kingdom of Israel went into captivity under the Assyrians! But Judah didn't heed that warning.

Why do we think we can deceive God and get away with it? Do we think God will exempt us from wholehearted obedience and fidelity to Him because we are His people? Do we think He would never allow the wicked to triumph over us because we profess Him and they don't?

Apparently that is what Judah thought, for when the false prophets proclaimed, "Peace, peace," the people loved what they said and believed their message (Jeremiah 5:30-31; 6:14). The temporary blessing and delayed judgment that came because of Josiah's repentance and obedience apparently lulled them into complacency, and they did not turn to God with all of their heart.

You may be hearing, "Peace, peace" . . . but is there peace deep within your heart? A peace which is not dependent upon your circumstances? If you want peace that the world cannot give and cannot take from you, make sure your relationship with God is what it ought to be. God must be your priority. Get rid of anything that hinders you from Him. When you refuse to give God first priority in your life, you deceive yourself.

What God spoke to Judah, He also speaks to you and me, for the things which were written before were written for our learning and admonition (see Romans 15:4). God told Judah,

"Return, O faithless sons, I will heal your faith-lessness. . . . If you will return, O Israel," declares the LORD, "Then you should return to Me. And if you will put away your detested things from My presence, and will not waver, and you will swear, 'As the LORD lives,' in truth, in justice, and in righteousness; then the nations will bless themselves in Him, and in Him they will glory."

For thus says the LORD to the men of Judah and to Jerusalem, "Break up your fallow ground, and do not sow among thorns. Circumcise your-selves to the LORD and remove the foreskins of your heart, men of Judah and inhabitants of Jerusalem, lest My wrath go forth like fire and burn with none to quench it, because of the evil of your deeds" (Jeremiah 3:22a;4:1-4).

In the space provided, list the things that are like fallow ground which need to be broken up within your heart—things which need to be circumcised or cut away so that your heart can beat unreservedly for Him.

DAY FIVE

When God finished speaking, Habakkuk knew he must wait quietly for the day of distress when the Babylonians would invade Judah (3:16b). Habakkuk knew that the people of Judah had been given ample opportunity to repent.

Listen again to Jeremiah:

JEREMIAH 7:1-28

The word that came to Jeremiah from the LORD, saying, "Stand in the gate of the LORD's house and proclaim there this word, and say, 'Hear the word of the LORD, all you of Judah, who enter by these gates to worship the LORD!'" Thus says the LORD of hosts, the God of Israel, "Amend your ways and your deeds, and I will let you dwell in this place. Do not trust in deceptive words, saying, 'This is the temple of the LORD, the temple of the LORD, the temple of the LORD.' For if you truly amend your ways and your deeds, if you truly practice justice between a man and his neighbor, if you do not oppress the alien, the orphan, or the widow, and do not shed innocent blood in this place, nor walk after other gods to your own ruin, then I will let you dwell in this place, in the land that I gave to your fathers forever and ever.

"Behold, you are trusting in deceptive words to no avail. Will you steal, murder, and commit adultery, and swear falsely, and offer sacrifices to Baal, and walk after other gods that you have not known, then come and stand before Me in this house, which is called by My name, and say, 'We are delivered!'—that you may do all these abominations? Has this house, which is called by My name, become a den of robbers in your sight? Behold, I, even I, have seen it," declares the LORD.

"But go now to My place which was in Shiloh, where I made My name dwell at the first, and see what I did to it because of the wickedness of My people Israel. And now, because you have done all these things," declares the LORD, "and I spoke to you, rising up early and speaking, but you did not hear, and I called you but you did not answer, therefore, I will do to the house which is called by My name, in which you trust, and to the place which I gave you and your fathers, as I did to Shiloh. And I will cast you out of My sight, as I have cast out all your brothers, all the offspring of Ephraim."

Eventually, events deteriorated to the point where God said to His prophet,

"As for you, do not pray for this people, and do not lift up cry or prayer for them, and do not intercede with Me; for I do not hear you. Do you not see what they are doing in the cities of Judah and in the streets of Jerusalem? The children gather wood, and the fathers kindle the fire, and the women knead dough to make cakes for the queen of heaven; and they pour out libations to other gods in order to spite Me. Do they spite Me?" declares the LORD. "Is it not themselves they spite, to their own shame?" Therefore thus says the Lord GOD, "Behold, My anger and My wrath will be poured out on this place, on man and on beast and on the trees of the field and on the fruit of the ground; and it will burn and not be quenched.

Thus says the LORD of hosts, the God of Israel, "Add your burnt offerings to your sacrifices and eat flesh. For I did not speak to your fathers, or command them in the day that I brought them out of the land of Egypt, concerning burnt offerings and sacrifices. But this is what I commanded them, saying, 'Obey My voice, and I will be your God, and you will be My people; and you will walk in all the way which I command you, that it may be well with you.' Yet they did not obey or incline their ear, but walked in their own counsels and in the stubbornness of their evil heart, and went backward and not forward. Since the day that your fathers came out of the land of Egypt until this day, I have sent you all My servants the prophets, daily rising early and sending them. Yet they did not listen to Me or incline their ear, but stiffened their neck; they did evil more than their fathers.

"And you shall speak all these words to them, but they will not listen to you; and you shall call to them, but they will not answer you. And you shall say to them, 'This is the nation that did not obey the voice of the LORD their God or accept correction; truth has perished and has been cut off from their mouth.'"

Now read through Jeremiah 7:1-28 again. This time make a list of what you learned about the people of Habakkuk and Jeremiah's day. As you do, put a star beside those things which parallel what is taking place in the country in which you live. Make a list of the things God told them to do, and a list of what God said He would do if they did not obey. [1]

"Truth has perished and has been cut off from their mouth." What a sad statement! Through truth we are sanctified—when we hear it and obey it.

That is why Jesus prayed for you and me, "Sanctify them in the truth; Thy word is truth" (John 17:17).

How has God sanctified you through His truth this week? Write it out below.

Hear the word of the Lord, amend your ways and your deeds; they walk in their own ways steal, murder. adultery
Obey my voice, and I be your God. and you will be your God and you will be my people and walk in all the ways I have command you that it may be well with you.

My anger and my wrath will be poured on you. justice and punishment will come
John 17-17. Thy Word is truth.

DAY SIX

Have you ever been in such anguish, such despair, such confusion that you felt you couldn't go on? Have you ever been overwhelmed with grief? Have you ever been angry—just plain angry—because of what was going on? Angry because you had no control over the situation? Or because of the injustice of it all? Or because what happened shouldn't have happened? And anger welled up within . . . maybe even at God?

What do you do in situations like these? How do you handle such feelings? How do you survive and come out on top as a conqueror rather than the conquered?

Christians are not exempt from such feelings. Even the spiritually mature can encounter such experiences. And yet, my friend, you don't have to allow these situations to capture you and cast you into a prison of despair. You need to do what Habakkuk did.

When overwhelmed, Habakkuk embraced God. Although his situation never changed as far as we know, he walked as a conqueror. With hinds' feet that did not slip, he walked above his circumstances on the high ground of faith (3:19).

The name *Habakkuk* means "one who embraces or caresses." When God seemed to ignore the sin of Judah, Habakkuk didn't bury his frustration with God. He expressed his anguish with God's seeming silence over all the iniquity he beheld. He didn't hide his feelings or questions under a cloak of spirituality. He didn't stuff them and deny that they burned in his heart. Rather, true to his name, Habakkuk brought it all out in the open and asked his Lord some hard questions. Then in faith he embraced what he knew about His covenant-keeping God and His Word.

And you, Beloved, need to do the same thing. Acknowledge where you are. (God knows anyway!)

Then, in faith, embrace what you know about your God.

Do you feel as if God doesn't hear your prayers? *yes*
Then cry out to Him and see how He answers through
our study in the days and weeks to come. God will
speak. He may not change your circumstances or
remove your burden, but through His Word, He will
bring you to the point where you can rejoice in Him
and find Him as your strength.

> I sought the LORD, and He answered me,
> And delivered me from all my fears.
> They looked to Him and were radiant,
> And their faces shall never be ashamed.
> This poor man cried and the LORD heard him,
> And saved him out of all his troubles
> (Psalm 34:4-6).

Don't you know how it touched the Father's heart
to have His son Habakkuk embrace Him in faith's
love? And say, in essence, "Father, I love You for Who
You are, not just for what You can do for me or for
what You will do for me. I love You no matter what . . .
and, Father, I will trust You. I know You love me."

Oh, my friend, will you embrace God in faith? Will
you caress Him in unconditional love? Will you please
Him with your faith? You were made in His image;
God experiences emotion just as you do. Will you be a
Habakkuk to your Father God? Tell Him right now. In
the space below, write out your prayer to Him.

thank you for your love and protecting
over us, in our stay in Hospital, for the Dead Drs
and nurses and Jadie + Sara who cared for me,
all the freinds and neighbors helped us.
God thank you for loving me, for what you
will do and I will trust you more. I confess
my sins, I love you Lord. and I might obey you
Thy Word is truth

45

DAY SEVEN

When bad things happen, God is always there. He is always in charge. However, many times we fail to realize this because we do not run to Him in faith. Although He may not always deliver as He does in the story I'm about to share, you will find His grace sufficient. This illustration is from a book you'll want to read for yourself: *Of Whom the World Is Not Worthy*, by Marie Chapian. A single story from its pages will show how one woman embraced God in faith.

A young, plump-cheeked Nazi policeman came to the women's cell one evening, eyeing the women smugly. He was not German, but a Jugoslav quisling who had defected to the Nazi side. He spoke Slovenian but with the typical bloated words of a person who had been a nobody all his life and now was important because of the importance of his associates. The brass Swastika at his throat gave him newly found stature and a puffed-up chest, the price of betraying his people.

He grinned at Jozeca and taunted, "We are shooting all of the old people who are of no use any longer."

"What do you mean?" demanded Jozeca.

The quisling guard looking directly at her and answered, "The old people, Frau, the old ones—especially the men, the men who have more than sixty years."

Jozeca bit her tongue. Jakob (her husband) had sixty-four years. *O God, have mercy.*

The fat-jowled guard licked his lips. "What good are old men over sixty anyhow, eh, Frau?"

She did not answer.

"Especially to the women. Ha Ha!"

She turned her head away.

"But my dear Frau, you need not trouble yourself. We will take care of you here. Ah, let it never be said that here in Stari Pisker we do not take care of our little neglected Fraus, eh! Such a young, ripe plum needs plucking. Do you not agree?"

He laughed and walked away, his fat sides wobbling. After he was gone, Jozeca began to tremble in anger, fear and horror. She raised her hands and clenched her fists.

"God! Look down upon me! Hear me!" And she prayed in a loud voice until she closed her eyes to sleep. Nobody stopped her. In fact, the women prayed with her. And before the morning sun rose, everyone in the cell knew that Jesus Christ was real and living and that in spite of every atrocity of man, He was a God of love.

It was about three o'clock in the morning when the fat guard came for her. With him were two other guards, both German. His chubby hands unsealed the lock of the cell door and he motioned for Jozeca to follow him. His face was pink and greasy in the pale green light. Jozeca did not move. The cell, heavy with the smells of perspiration, tears and human excretion, was silent. The fish smell from the day before still lingered on the women's clothes and hair.

Again he motioned for her to follow him. She did not move. He entered the cell and took her arm. As he touched her, he recoiled as though burned. "Acht!"

He grabbed her arm again, and again he recoiled.

"Devil!" he snarled.

"Jesus!" she answered.

He stood glowering at her and she remained unmoving. His face was a deeper pink. He pulled out his Luger and pointed it at her temple. Then he laughed nervously and wiped his wet mouth with his hand.

"Now you will come, Frau," he said.

She looked him straight in the eye and did not move. He cocked the hammer of the gun.

"Move! Now!"

Jozeca's eyes narrowed as she kept them on the quisling Nazi. He pressed the gun to her head and then he suddenly recoiled again as though singed by fire.

"Devil!" he cursed.

"Jesus," she repeated.

He humphed and grunted and jammed the gun back into his leather holster. Then with his high, black boots squeaking beneath him, he turned to leave the cell. The two guards with him snickered at him.

His pride deeply wounded, he angrily twirled around and told Jozeca, "Tomorrow you will be shot!"

Jozeca immediately raised her hands to heaven and praised God. "O God! Jesus! Dear Holy Spirit! You have delivered me from the destroyer! Praise the name of the Lord! O God! Thank You, Lord! Thank You with my soul! And if You would will it so that I once again will see my son and my husband, do not allow me to die tomorrow."

She slept peacefully that night. There were no

shots heard in the courtyard during the entire month they were in the prison. And that month not one person over sixty years of age was killed. [2]

Notes

1. When you complete this, you may want to record the information in the margin of Jeremiah 7 in your *International Inductive Study Bible*.

2. Marie Chapian, *Of Whom the World Was Not Worthy* (Minneapolis, Minnesota: Bethany Fellowship, 1978), 100-101.

Chapter 3

HE'S THERE,
HE HASN'T LEFT HIS
SOVEREIGN THRONE

When God doesn't seem to hear your cries or answer your prayers, you need to remember five principles. We will explore each one so you might fully understand them and hide them in your heart. These truths will hold you in times of darkness, in times of trial and testing.

1. *God is in control. He rules over all. He's in charge of history.*

2. *All history centers or pivots on two groups of people: Israel and the Church.*

3. *Whether or not we see it or understand it, there is a purpose in what God is doing.*

4. *Our times are in His hands.*

5. *Fear and doubt are conquered by a faith that rejoices.*

Listen to Habakkuk in chapter three:

Though the fig tree should not blossom,
And there be no fruit on the vines,
Though the yield of the olive should fail,
And the fields produce no food,
Though the flock should be cut off from the
    fold,
And there be no cattle in the stalls,
Yet I will exult in the LORD,
I will rejoice in the God of my salvation.
The Lord GOD is my strength,
And He has made my feet like hinds' feet,
And makes me walk on my high places
                (Habakkuk 3:17-19).

What confidence, trust, love, commitment! In all the Word of God, there is no greater declaration of faith. Habakkuk asked God hard questions. When God answered, Habakkuk submitted to Him in faith.

What enables a man or woman to make such a pledge of allegiance? It is the understanding of Who God is and the realization that He is sovereign—that He accomplishes His plan, that nothing keeps Him from achieving His purpose.

My prayer for you and for me is that Habakkuk 3:17-19 will become our unwavering declaration of faith. Your assignment for today is to memorize these verses so they will be written forever on the pages of your heart. If you'll read them aloud three times a day soon you'll find yourself able to quote them. Also, if you'll draw a simple sketch of what they say, you'll find it will help you remember their message.

Finally, take a few moments to meditate on the message of Isaiah 50:8-10:

> He who vindicates Me is near;
> Who will contend with Me?
> Let us stand up to each other;
> Who has a case against Me?
> Let him draw near to Me.
> Behold, the Lord GOD helps Me;
> Who is he who condemns Me?
> Behold, they will all wear out like a garment;
> The moth will eat them.
> Who is among you that fears the LORD,
> That obeys the voice of His servant,
> That walks in darkness and has no light?
> Let him trust in the name of the LORD
> and rely on his God.

DAY TWO

God is in control. He rules over all. He's in charge of history. Habakkuk asked God why He didn't hear his cry for help, why He let him see iniquity, violence, and destruction, and why He didn't deliver the righteous when He saw violence. Habakkuk couldn't understand why God allowed the wicked to surround the righteous and permitted justice to be perverted. God answered by assuring Habakkuk that He was in control.

Listen to Habakkuk 1:5: "Look among the nations! Observe! Be astonished! Wonder! Because I am doing something in your days—you would not believe if you were told."

Although Habakkuk hadn't seen it yet, God *was* doing something: He was raising up the Babylonians, a fierce, heathen nation He would eventually use for His glorious eternal purpose. He knew and understood the iniquity, injustice, strife, and violence. And He was going to do something about it. Hard though it would be for Habakkuk to understand, God was going to use the Babylonians to judge His people Judah! God is in charge of history and, thus, rules over the nations.

This may present problems for you as you remember the many atrocities that men or nations have inflicted upon their fellow men—the insane cruelties of Hitler as he exterminated millions of Jews or the communist purges of the Chinese as they moved across that land. But please don't just close this book and walk away. Hear me out as I share with you what the Word of God teaches about God's sovereignty.

I believe that it was an understanding of the sovereignty of God that enabled Habakkuk to say what he did in Habakkuk 3:17-19. In Habakkuk 3:19, he used the name "Lord GOD" to describe God. There the Hebrew word for "Lord" is *Adonai*, which means "master, ruler." The Hebrew word for "GOD" is *YHWH*, and is the most sacred of all the names of God.

Therefore, when you combine these two names, *Adonai Yahweh* (Jehovah), it could be translated as the New International Version translates it: Sovereign Lord.

Oh, Beloved, when you can't understand what is going on and how God can allow such iniquity to exist without immediately intervening, you need to rest in the truth of God's sovereignty. No other truth has so sustained me through all my trials and testings.

Read Isaiah 14:24-27. God was going to judge the northern kingdom of Israel by allowing Assyria to invade them and take them captive. This was His plan for judging Israel's sin. What God plans and purposes He brings to pass. No one, nothing can thwart Him. Remember that. Write out verses 24 and 27 in the space that follows, and memorize them. They'll hold you and comfort you in the days ahead.

DAY THREE

I wasn't saved until I was twenty-nine years old. By then, I was a mess—a poor representative of what God intended a woman to be.

I wanted to be perfect, but I wasn't.

I tried to be good, but I couldn't.

I thought I was a Christian, but I wasn't.

I was merely *religious*.

The one thing I wanted in life—to be happily married—had eluded me. The perfect marriage, the perfect family, the perfect home were dreams that never became reality.

At twenty-nine I was a divorcee with two precious sons. It was a divorce of my own doing. But it was the undoing of me. Without the restraints of marriage and consumed by a passion to be loved, I became an immoral woman.

Finally, I saw myself as I really was: a slave to sin.

On July 16, 1963, I came to know the Lord Jesus Christ and became a new creature. How awed I was by the changes the Holy Spirit made in my life! Next to being able to say no to sin, the greatest excitement was in reading God's Word and being able to understand it. I did not know at the time that this is the birthright of every child of God (1 Corinthians 2:9-16).

After I came to know Jesus Christ, God sent a godly man to tutor me in the faith. I was like a dry sponge being softened by the Word, absorbing all that I could get. One night as Dave and I sat in my living room, he took off his signet ring and put it into his hand, clinching his fingers around it until his knuckles were white. Then he said, "Kay, now that you belong to Jesus Christ, you are just like this ring, and my hand is just like the hand of God. God has you in His hand. No one can touch you, look at you, or speak to you without God's permission."

I didn't recognize it then, but Dave was teaching me the sovereignty of God. Later as I came to understand that God is sovereign—in control of all so that nothing can happen without His knowledge or permission—I understood more fully what Dave was saying. I also understood that the God who held me in His sovereign hand is a God of love (1 John 4:10). Everything that came into my life would have to be filtered through His fingers of love.

"Filtered through fingers of love" became a phrase I would pass down to my students to cling to through their trials.

When I wanted to marry Dave and counselors told him not to marry me because I was divorced, I clung to this truth.

When I told God I'd go back and marry my ex-husband, and then he committed suicide, I clung to this truth.

God is in control. He rules over all. He loves me. He desires my highest good.

Oh, dear child of God, do you see that no matter what happens in your life, in your family, or in your nation, you, like Habakkuk, can rejoice in the God of your salvation? Everything in your life is filtered through His fingers of love.

And how will it end? Read Romans 8:28-30 and write out your answer on the next page.

56

He's There, He Hasn't Left His Sovereign Throne

DAY FOUR

Daniel 4:34-35 offers one of the clearest statements of God's sovereignty in all of Scripture. Let's examine it in the light of its context and see how it relates to Habakkuk and to the principle we need to remember in times of distress: **God is in control. He rules over the nations. He's in charge of history.**

God, you'll remember, told Habakkuk that it was He who was "raising up the Chaldeans, that fierce and impetuous people" who would march throughout the earth to seize dwelling places and to eventually correct Judah for her sin (Habakkuk 1:6, 12). The book of Daniel begins with an account of the beginning of the "day of distress." This was the day Habakkuk was to quietly anticipate as he waited "for the people to arise who will invade us" (Habakkuk 3:16).

The book of Daniel begins, "In the third year of the reign of Jehoiakim king of Judah, Nebuchadnezzar king of Babylon came to Jerusalem and besieged it. And the Lord *gave* Jehoiakim king of Judah into his hand" (Daniel 1:1-2; emphasis added). God *gave* Jehoiakim over to the Babylonians just as He told Habakkuk He would.

There were three sieges of Jerusalem before it was finally taken captive in 586 B.C. Daniel was taken captive in the first siege. Shortly afterward King Nebuchadnezzar came to realize and recognize the sovereignty of God. Daniel 4, either dictated or handwritten by the king, tells how he came to acknowledge God's sovereignty.

Daniel chapter 4 is printed out for you. Mark each reference to the following words as well as the appropriate synonyms and pronouns for each one:

1. God

2. Nebuchadnezzar

3. Daniel and/or Belteshazzar

Nebuchadnezzar the king to all the peoples, nations, and men of every language that live in all the earth: "May your peace abound! It has seemed good to me to declare the signs and wonders which the Most High God has done for me.

How great are His signs,
And how mighty are His wonders!
His kingdom is an everlasting kingdom,
And His dominion is from generation to
  generation.

"I, Nebuchadnezzar, was at ease in my house and flourishing in my palace. I saw a dream and it made me fearful; and these fantasies as I lay on my bed and the visions in my mind kept alarming me. So I gave orders to bring into my presence all the wise men of Babylon, that they might make known to me the interpretation of the dream. Then the magicians, the conjurers, the Chaldeans, and the diviners came in, and I related the dream to them; but they could not make its interpretation known to me. But finally Daniel came in before me, whose name is Belteshazzar according to the name of my god, and in whom is a spirit of the holy gods; and I related the dream to him, saying, 'O Belteshazzar, chief of the magicians, since I know that a spirit of the holy gods is in you and no mystery baffles you, tell me the visions of my dream which I have seen, along with its interpretation. Now these were the visions in my mind as I lay on my bed: I was looking, and behold, there was a tree in the midst of the earth, and its height was great.

'The tree grew large and became strong,
And its height reached to the sky,

And it was visible to the end of the whole
   earth.
Its foliage was beautiful and its fruit abundant,
And in it was food for all.
The beasts of the field found shade under it,
And the birds of the sky dwelt in its branches,
And all living creatures fed themselves from it.
'I was looking in the visions in my mind as I
   lay on my bed, and behold, an angelic
   watcher, a holy one, descended from
   heaven.
'He shouted out and spoke as follows:
"Chop down the tree and cut off its branches,
Strip off its foliage and scatter its fruit;
Let the beasts flee from under it,
And the birds from its branches.
Yet leave the stump with its roots in the
   ground,
But with a band of iron and bronze around it
In the new grass of the field;
And let him be drenched with the dew of
   heaven,
And let him share with the beasts in the grass
   of the earth.
Let his mind be changed from that of a man,
And let a beast's mind be given to him,
And let seven periods of time pass over him.
This sentence is by the decree of the angelic
   watchers,
And the decision is a command of the holy
   ones,
In order that the living may know
That the Most High is ruler over the realm of
   mankind,
And bestows it on whom He wishes,
And sets over it the lowliest of men."

'This is the dream which I, King Nebuchadnezzar,
have seen. Now you, Belteshazzar, tell me its
interpretation, inasmuch as none of the wise

men of my kingdom is able to make known to
me the interpretation; but you are able, for a
spirit of the holy gods is in you.'

"Then Daniel, whose name is Belteshazzar, was
appalled for a while as his thoughts alarmed
him. The king responded and said,
'Belteshazzar, do not let the dream or its interpretation alarm you.' Belteshazzar answered and
said, 'My lord, if only the dream applied to
those who hate you, and its interpretation to
your adversaries! The tree that you saw, which
became large and grew strong, whose height
reached to the sky and was visible to all the
earth, and whose foliage was beautiful and its
fruit abundant, and in which was food for all,
under which the beasts of the field dwelt and in
whose branches the birds of the sky lodged—it
is you, O king; for you have become great and
grown strong, and your majesty has become
great and reached to the sky and your dominion
to the end of the earth. And in that the king saw
an angelic watcher, a holy one, descending from
heaven and saying, "Chop down the tree and
destroy it; yet leave the stump with its roots in
the ground, but with a band of iron and bronze
around it in the new grass of the field, and let
him be drenched with the dew of heaven, and
let him share with the beasts of the field until
seven periods of time pass over him"; this is the
interpretation, O king, and this is the decree of
the Most High, which has come upon my lord
the king: that you be driven away from
mankind, and your dwelling place be with the
beasts of the field, and you be given grass to eat
like cattle and be drenched with the dew of
heaven; and seven periods of time will pass
over you, until you recognize that the Most High
is ruler over the realm of mankind, and bestows
it on whomever He wishes. And in that it was

commanded to leave the stump with the roots of the tree, your kingdom will be assured to you after you recognize that it is Heaven that rules. Therefore, O king, may my advice be pleasing to you: break away now from your sins by doing righteousness, and from your iniquities by showing mercy to the poor, in case there may be a prolonging of your prosperity.'

"All this happened to Nebuchadnezzar the king. Twelve months later he was walking on the roof of the royal palace of Babylon. The king reflected and said, 'Is this not Babylon the great, which I myself have built as a royal residence by the might of my power and for the glory of my majesty?' While the word was in the king's mouth, a voice came from heaven, saying, 'King Nebuchadnezzar, to you it is declared: sovereignty has been removed from you, and you will be driven away from mankind, and your dwelling place will be with the beasts of the field. You will be given grass to eat like cattle, and seven periods of time will pass over you, until you recognize that the Most High is ruler over the realm of mankind, and bestows it on whomever He wishes.' Immediately the word concerning Nebuchadnezzar was fulfilled; and he was driven away from mankind and began eating grass like cattle, and his body was drenched with the dew of heaven, until his hair had grown like eagles' feathers and his nails like birds' claws.

"But at the end of that period I, Nebuchadnezzar, raised my eyes toward heaven, and my reason returned to me, and I blessed the Most High and praised and honored Him who lives forever;

"For His dominion is an everlasting dominion,
And His kingdom endures from generation to
    generation.

And all the inhabitants of the earth are accounted
    as nothing,
But He does according to His will in the host
    of heaven
And among the inhabitants of earth;
And no one can ward off His hand
Or say to Him, 'What hast Thou done?'

"At that time my reason returned to me. And
my majesty and splendor were restored to me
for the glory of my kingdom, and my counselors and my nobles began seeking me out; so
I was reestablished in my sovereignty, and sur-
passing greatness was added to me. Now I
Nebuchadnezzar praise, exalt, and honor the
King of heaven, for all His works are true and
His ways just, and He is able to humble those
who walk in pride."

Tomorrow we will look more closely at the truths
of Daniel 4.

DAY FIVE

Nebuchadnezzar was given a dream from God "in order that the living may know that the Most High is ruler over the realm of mankind, and bestows it on whom He wishes, and sets over it the lowliest of men" (Daniel 4:17b).

God spoke very clearly about His sovereignty to Nebuchadnezzar, not only through a dream, but also through a clear and frightening interpretation. Yet it didn't sink in:

"Twelve months later he was walking on the roof of the royal palace of Babylon. The king reflected and said, 'Is this not Babylon the great, which I myself have built as a royal residence by the might of my power and for the glory of my majesty?'" (Daniel 4:29-30).

Nebuchadnezzar isn't much different from other men, is he? We think we are the captains of our fate. We think we determine our own destiny. We forget that "every good thing bestowed and every perfect gift is from above, coming down from the Father of lights" (James 1:17) and that God "does according to His will in the host of heaven and among the inhabitants of earth" (Daniel 4:35).

Read through Daniel chapter 4 again, noting the references you marked yesterday to Nebuchadnezzar, Daniel, and God.

1. In the space provided, list what you learn from this chapter about Nebuchadnezzar. You might want to categorize your thoughts according to the three major events in the chapter:

a. The dream

b. The interpretation

c. The events that occurred twelve months later

2. Now list everything you learn about God from Daniel 4.

God is in control of history; it's *His story*. Doesn't that give you great peace—especially when world events seems so tumultuous and insane?

DAY SIX

After God humbled Nebuchadnezzar by letting him lose his mind, He brought the king back to his senses. As a result, Nebuchadnezzar wrote these words about God: "For His dominion is an everlasting dominion, and His kingdom endures from generation to generation. And all the inhabitants of the earth are accounted as nothing, but He does according to His will in the host of heaven and among the inhabitants of earth;

65

and no one can ward off His hand or say to Him, 'What hast Thou done?'" (Daniel 4:34b-35).

Oh, Beloved, God is telling us He rules over all that is in heaven and on earth. This includes not only the cherubim, the seraphim, and the good angels, but He also rules over every demon and over the prince of the power of the air, Satan himself! This means that neither Satan nor his demons can ever do anything to you apart from God's permission.

I want you to take a few minutes and look up the following verses. Record any insights you learn about God's sovereignty.

1. Luke 22:31-32

2. 1 Corinthians 10:13

3. Romans 8:35-39

4. Genesis 50:20

Remember when Jesus told Peter that he would deny Him? It was at this time that Jesus said, "Simon, Simon, behold, Satan has demanded permission to sift you like wheat; but I have prayed for you, that your faith may not fail" (Luke 22:31-32). Do you see the sovereignty of God over Satan? *Satan had to get God's permission to sift Peter!* Can you see the implication of that truth in your own life? Satan can never do anything to you without God's permission. Therefore, according to 1 Corinthians 10:13, whatever comes into your life will never be more than you can bear! Wow! No wonder you can be more than a conqueror through Jesus Christ in every circumstance of life (Romans 8:35-39)!

Not only is it true that you can live as a conqueror, but since God does according to His will among the inhabitants of the earth, then no one on earth can do anything to you without God's permission. This truth means that no human being can overpower or surprise God. This truth also shows why you can rejoice in God no matter what. "In everything give thanks; for this is God's will for you in Christ Jesus" (1 Thessalonians 5:18).

Because God is sovereign, He can promise that *all* things will work together for good for those who love Him, for those who are called according to *His purpose.* For those whom He foreknows, He predestines to become conformed to the image of His Son (Romans 8:28-29). Because God is sovereign, even when people intend to do evil against you, God will work it out for your good. He is the Redeemer of the difficulties, trials, and tragedies of life.

Joseph understood this. Although his jealous brothers sold him into slavery, smeared blood on his beautiful multicolored coat, and told their father that he had been killed, Joseph did not nurse a grudge against them in bitter anger. Instead, when he had the power to imprison and dispose of them, he said, "As for you, you meant evil against me, but God meant it for good in order to bring about this present result, to preserve many people alive" (Genesis 50:20).

Isn't understanding God's sovereignty exciting? Awesome? Comforting? Are you understanding more

He's There, He Hasn't Left His Sovereign Throne

clearly why Habakkuk could say what he did in 3:17-19? No matter what happens, because God is sovereign, you can live above it all with hinds' feet on high places—if you are His child.

Have you ever had to deal with questions like these:

If God is sovereign, are men still responsible for what they do?

Why does a sovereign God allow men to do evil?

Why does God allow men to suffer because of the unrighteousness of others?

Let's begin to answer these questions by looking at Isaiah 45:5-7. These verses are in a section of prophecy given about Cyrus the king of the Persians, who would be born 175 years later.

1. Write out Isaiah 45:7.

2. What do you learn about God from Isaiah 45:5-7? Write it out.

Does a sovereign God hold men accountable for the evil they do, even though God uses their evil to accomplish His purpose?

Yes.

God told Habakkuk that it was He who was raising up the Babylonians to correct Judah (1:5-6,12). Yet, even though God raised them up as His rod of judgment, He would hold the Babylonians guilty (1:11). In fact, in Habakkuk 2:6-20 God pronounced judgments that were going to come upon evil men, the Babylonians in particular.

How well this parallels Matthew 18:7: "Woe to the world because of its stumbling blocks! For it is inevitable that stumbling blocks come; but woe to that man through whom the stumbling block comes!" There is going to be evil in the world, but God will use that evil to accomplish His purpose. Yet, He will hold evil men accountable!

Let's look at one more Scripture that illustrates this thought. When our Lord stood before Pilate, Pilate said to Him, "Do You not know that I have authority to release You, and I have authority to crucify You?" (John 19:10). To which Jesus answered, "You would have no authority over Me, unless it had been given you from above; for this reason he who delivered Me up to you has the greater sin" (John 19:11).

In other words, all that happened to Jesus in His trial and death were under God's control. Those who betrayed Him and sentenced Him to death, however, would still be held accountable.

Our second question was, "Why does a sovereign God allow men to do evil?" Habakkuk asked this question in 1:12-17. We will answer it in greater detail when we look at our second principle, but right now let me simply say that God allows men to be evil in order to accomplish His purpose. Remember what you learned in Isaiah 45:5-7? You saw that God is "the One forming light and creating darkness, causing well-being and creating calamity."

Our third question was, "Why does God allow the righteous to suffer at the hands of the unrighteous?" Habakkuk asked the same thing in 1:13. You will see the answer to this question more fully in the days to come. Remember, there is a purpose in what God is doing, whether we see it or not. Nothing is going to hinder God's plan for executing that purpose.

Remember Isaiah 14:24 and 27? You memorized those verses earlier in this study.

Now then, what is God's lesson for us? Although God causes all things to work together for good for His children, He still holds us accountable for our behavior. *The sovereignty of God never lets us off the hook. God still holds us responsible for our actions.* It is important that you remember this. When some learn of the sovereignty of God, they fold their arms and say, "What will be, will be." With that attitude, they do nothing, or excuse their behavior on the basis of their unbalanced understanding of God's sovereignty.

But what about you, my friend? What is your response to the sovereignty of God? Write it out below in the form of a prayer to your sovereign Lord.

Once you understand *and* embrace what the Bible teaches about the character and sovereignty of God, you will find calm in the center of life's storms.

To know that God rules over all—that there are no accidents in life, that no tactic of Satan or man can ever thwart the will of God—brings divine comfort.

Then it is easy to understand how the promise of Romans 8:28-30 can be true: "And we know that God causes all things to work together for good to those who love God, to those who are called according to His purpose. For whom He foreknew, He also predestined to become conformed to the image of His Son, that He might be the first-born among many brethren; and whom He predestined, these He also called; and whom He called, these He also justified; and whom He justified, these He also glorified."

He's There, He Hasn't Left His Sovereign Throne

When you grasp and bow to the truth of how all things are working together for good to conform you to His image, then in faith you are able to rejoice and give thanks in all things, knowing that this is the will of God in Christ Jesus concerning you (1 Thessalonians 5:18).

Stop right now and thank Him in faith.

Chapter 4

HE'S THERE,
REMEMBER WHO HE IS

DAY ONE

What kind of a God allows barbaric, cruel, godless men to dominate nations and wage war?

If God is sovereign and if God is love, why does He permit horrible calamities and gruesome tragedies?

If you've been thinking such thoughts, don't be ashamed. These questions must be answered, for it is only in answering them that you will be able to find peace and rest.

Habakkuk had to deal with those questions. He, too, was troubled. Habakkuk did what you and I must do when things are too hard for us to reconcile, to understand, and therefore, to accept. We, like Habakkuk, must go back to what we know God's Word says about God. Stop and read Habakkuk 1 again and see how Habakkuk discovers this in his conversation with God.

In 1:12, Habakkuk filtered through his mind the character of a God who would allow such things. He rehearsed the attributes of God. In doing so, he was able to walk in faith—even though he couldn't fully understand how and why God was doing what He was doing. Watch carefully what Habakkuk did. There will come a time, Beloved, when you will need to do likewise. It may even be now.

In Habakkuk 1:12-13a, the prophet said,

"Art Thou not from everlasting,
O LORD, my God, my Holy One?
We will not die.
Thou, O LORD, hast appointed them to judge;
And Thou, O Rock, hast established them to
    correct.
Thine eyes are too pure to approve evil,
And Thou canst not look on wickedness with
    favor."

What did Habakkuk call to mind about God?

First, he remembered that God is *eternal.* Look up the following verses and record what you learn about the eternity of God.

1. Psalm 90:1-2

2. 1 Timothy 6:15-16

3. Deuteronomy 33:27

4. Isaiah 40:28

God is from everlasting to everlasting—the beginning and the end (Revelation 21:6). He always has been, and He always will be. If He is eternal, then all things find their beginning and end in Him. "All things came into being by Him; and apart from Him nothing came into being that has come into being" (John 1:3). "For from Him and through Him and to Him are all things" (Romans 11:36a).

One thing will always remain: God. And because He is immutable (unchanging), He will always be the same. Your husband, wife, children, parents, and loved ones may be taken away, but God will always be there. He will never leave you nor forsake you (Hebrews 13:5).

Oh, friend, don't you see? No matter what the changes in your life, in your family, in your nation, there is always one stabilizing factor in which you can rest: your God. He is the immovable Rock. You can hide in Him.

He is always there with arms open wide, your everlasting Father God.

The eternity of God was the first attribute that Habakkuk called to mind. Precious child of God, why don't you simply meditate on the fact that although your history may change, God will not? He is everlasting. He can bring stability to your life. Claim that in faith.

DAY TWO

Not only is God everlasting, He is also *self-existent.* This is what the term LORD implies. YHWH (Yahweh), usually rendered "LORD" in the New American Standard Bible, is the most sacred of God's names. This is the name of God that reveals Him as the great I AM, the self-existent One, for YHWH is derived from the Hebrew verb *hayah,* which means "to be."

Take a few minutes and read Exodus 3. If you have an *International Inductive Study Bible,* you'll find it profitable to work through that chapter according to the instructions under *THINGS TO DO.*

When God appeared to Moses at the burning bush and told him He was sending him to deliver the Israelites from the land of Egypt, from the house of bondage, Moses responded to God,

"Behold, I am going to the sons of Israel, and I shall say to them, 'The God of your fathers has sent me to you.' Now they may say to me, 'What is His name?' What shall I say to them?" And God said to Moses, "I AM WHO I AM"; and He said, "'Thus you shall say to the sons of Israel, 'I AM has sent me to you.'" And God, furthermore, said to Moses, "Thus you shall say to the sons of Israel, 'The LORD, the God of your fathers, the God of Abraham, the God of Isaac, and the God of Jacob, has sent me to you.' This is My name forever, and this is My memorial-name to all generations" (Exodus 3:13-15).

If I AM is God's memorial-name to all generations, then that includes *your* generation as well! He is *your* great I AM—"I AM everything and anything you will ever need." Isn't that exciting? If we would only believe it and live accordingly.

"The name of the LORD is a strong tower; the righteous runs into it and is safe," says Proverbs 18:10. This is exactly what Habakkuk did when he reminded himself of who God is. Focusing on who God is enabled Habakkuk to live as more than a conqueror in very dark days. How clear this is in Habakkuk 3:18, when the prophet declared in faith, "Yet I will exult in the LORD, I will rejoice in the God of my salvation." Once again he used the name YHWH, the great I AM.

Habakkuk's existence and welfare did not depend on fig trees, fruit, olives, fields yielding crops, or on cattle in the stalls. His existence depended on his YHWH, the self-existent I AM. I AM would always be there as Habakkuk's strength, giving him hinds' feet that would not slip. His I AM would enable him to live above his circumstances, whatever they might be.

Because God does not change, He will do the same for you. He is to you as He was to Habakkuk—everything you will ever need, your I AM. You will discover this moment by moment as you exult in Who He is!

I want you, Beloved (and you are Beloved), to do as 2 Corinthians 13:5 says: "Test yourselves to see if you are in the faith; examine yourselves! Or do you not recognize this about yourselves, that Jesus Christ is in you—unless indeed you fail the test?"

Test your faith. Ask God to examine your heart. See if His Spirit bears witness with your spirit that you are a child of God (Romans 8:16).

DAY THREE

Life may seem so frustrating, overwhelming, and futile to you right now that you're tempted to check out.

Maybe you have thought of walking away, running away, leaving it all—maybe having an affair or getting a divorce. Have you been tempted to forget holiness and pursue happiness or to compromise your convictions because it doesn't seem to do you any good to live righteously? Maybe you feel your convictions have just left you poor or lonely. Maybe you are thinking of selling out to the pressure and saying yes. Or maybe you're thinking of just ending it all, escaping in death's sweet peace. But will it be peace—or hell?

Maybe . . . maybe . . . maybe.

Do you ever think maybes like these? It's not healthy, my friend. The Bible calls these "imaginations" or "speculations" (2 Corinthians 10:5). If they get hold of you, they can devastate or destroy you.

As 2 Corinthians 10:3-6 teaches, you are in a warfare, and the warfare is for your mind. As a man thinks in his heart, so he is (Proverbs 23:7). The enemy of your soul, the devil, knows this. That's why he targets your mind with his poison arrows. Satan wants you to think contrary to the character and the Word of God. His tactics are to accuse God and others. He wants to persuade you to act independently of God, to walk according to the flesh rather than the Spirit.

Maybes are lies. They are Satan's alternatives to total obedience to God's Word. They are shortcuts to happiness that, if pursued by man, bring only misery—a living hell.

You must do as Habakkuk did. The cure for maybes is to focus on the certainties of the character of your God and, in faith, to embrace all that He is. Bring every thought captive to the obedience of Jesus Christ by casting down imaginations and every high thought that is raised up against the knowledge of God (2 Corinthians 10:5).

Habakkuk went to God.

The prophet reminded God and himself that God was from everlasting, that He was Jehovah, his God, his Holy One. Does God mind when we remind Him of who He is? No! This delights Him. Moses, Jehoshaphat, David, and other great men and women of faith did the same.

1. Look at how Moses appealed to his Lord God in Exodus 32:11-13. What did Moses remind God of in this passage?

2. Now look at what Jehoshaphat said to the LORD in 2 Chronicles 20:6-12, and note what you learn.

Join Moses and Jehoshaphat! Plead your case in the light of His character. Turn from your maybes to the certainties of God. Like Habakkuk, you will find God to be your strength.

Don't allow a maybe to capture your attention. Instead, focus on God: His holiness, His faithfulness, His sufficiency, His veracity. Then you will have His strength so that you won't have to check out, walk out, or give up in despair.

When Habakkuk was troubled with God's seeming deafness to his cries and agony, he did not turn to ungodly maybes. As I said before, ungodly maybes are man's alternatives for submitting to God, for pleasing Him. They are the flesh's way of escape. They are you saying to God, "If this is what I have to endure, then maybe I'll . . . take things into my own hands, get a divorce, run away, cheat, lie, steal, indulge myself, compromise, and so on."

Instead, Habakkuk remembered that the Lord was his *Elohim.* Habakkuk said, "Art Thou not from everlasting, O LORD, my God, my Holy One?" (Habakkuk 1:12). *Elohim,* the Hebrew word for "God" in Habakkuk 1:12, is the name used for God in His role as Creator.

As you focus on God as Elohim, you are reminded in Hebrews 11:3 that "the worlds were prepared by the word of God, so that what is seen was not made out of things which are visible." God is the One Who is in control, the One Whose Word is so powerful that it brought a universe into existence. If God with a word can create the universe, can He not also subdue all things by the Word of His power when He is ready to do so? Of course!

As Elohim, He created all things. "All things have been created by Him and for Him" (Colossians 1:16). Because of this truth, my friend, maybes are not our rightful option. Rather, we are called to submission. No matter what happens, we need to say, "Father, I exist because of You and for You. Therefore, not my will but Yours be done."

Would it do us any good to fight against God? To raise our puny fists in the face of Omnipotence and say, "What are You doing?" Would He need to answer us? Does He need to consult with us? Does God exist for us . . . or do we exist for Him? Can we choose our parents? Add inches to our height? Change the color of our eyes or skin? Do we know how long we will live? Can we lengthen our days? Can we keep ourselves alive if Elohim decides to take away our breath? Can we determine our destiny? If we say there is no life beyond the grave, does that mean there is none?

Take a few minutes to look up the following scriptures and see God's answers to these questions.

1. Psalm 103:19

2. Revelation 4:11

3. Psalm 139:13-16

4. Job 12:10

5. Hebrews 9:27

6. Revelation 20:11-15; Isaiah 66:24

Paul wrote,

> Oh, the depth of the riches both of the wisdom
> and knowledge of God! How unsearchable are
> His judgments and unfathomable His ways! For
> WHO HAS KNOWN THE MIND OF THE LORD, OR WHO
> HAS BECOME HIS COUNSELOR? Or WHO HAS FIRST GIVEN
> TO HIM THAT IT MIGHT BE PAID BACK TO HIM AGAIN?
> For from Him and through Him and to Him are
> all things. To Him be the glory forever. Amen.
>
> I urge you therefore, brethren, by the mercies
> of God, to present your bodies a living and
> holy sacrifice, acceptable to God, which is your
> spiritual service of worship. And do not be con-
> formed to this world, but be transformed by the
> renewing of your mind, that you may prove
> what the will of God is, that which is good and
> acceptable and perfect (Romans 11:33-12:2).

DAY FOUR

Not only is God the self-existent Creator, He is also
the Holy One of Israel. This Habakkuk brought to
God's remembrance when God informed him that He
would judge Judah. When Satan's fiery darts are aimed
at your mind, rehearse God's holiness. So often when
things go wrong, man wants to blame God. But can a
holy God do what is wrong?

Holiness is total purity without any taint of evil or
wrongdoing. And what makes God holy? It is the sum
total of all of His attributes, making Him totally other

than man. Because God is holy, He can do no wrong. If He did, He would not be holy. Therefore, whatever Habakkuk's conception of what God was doing in allowing such evil to abound, he knew it could not contradict the truth he knew about God. And Habakkuk knew that God was holy! Habakkuk could not judge God as being unjust in what His sovereignty permitted.

And neither can you, my friend. If you'll remember that, you'll walk in faith and save yourself a lot of grief.

In reminding God of Who He was, Habakkuk saw that it was because of God's holiness that He was allowing the Babylonians to correct Judah. "Art Thou not from everlasting, O LORD, my God, my Holy One? We will not die. Thou, O LORD, hast appointed them to judge; and Thou, O Rock, hast established them to correct" (Habakkuk 1:12).

This is another reason why you cannot consider ungodly maybes. If you do, whether a child of God or not, God in His holiness will have to correct you even as He had to correct Judah. "For it is time for judgment to begin with the household of God; and if it begins with us first, what will be the outcome for those who do not obey the gospel of God?" (1 Peter 4:17).

Why did Habakkuk know that they would not die even though God would judge them in righteousness? What did Habakkuk mean by the term "die"? Surely when the Babylonians went up against God's chosen in battle, people would die!

Yes, some would die physically; but as a nation, Israel would not die—the nation would not be wiped out. This, I believe, is what Habakkuk meant. Habakkuk knew that God was immutable; He would not change. Habakkuk knew that His God was a covenant-keeping God.

For example, on the day that Abraham believed God, Abraham wanted assurance from God that he and his descendants would forever possess the land of Canaan. So when Abraham asked God, "O Lord GOD, how may I know that I shall possess it?" (Genesis 15:8), God said to him,

> "Bring Me a three year old heifer, and a three year old female goat, and a three year old ram, and a turtledove, and a young pigeon." Then he brought all these to Him and cut them in two, and laid each half opposite the other; but he did not cut the birds. And the birds of prey came down upon the carcasses, and Abram drove them away.[1]
>
> Now when the sun was going down, a deep sleep fell upon Abram; and behold, terror and great darkness fell upon him. And God said to Abram, "Know for certain that your descendants will be strangers in a land that is not theirs, where they will be enslaved and oppressed four hundred years. But I will also judge the nation whom they will serve; and afterward they will come out with many possessions. And as for you, you shall go to your fathers in peace; you shall be buried at a good old age. Then in the fourth generation they shall return here, for the iniquity of the Amorite is not yet complete." And it came about when the sun had set, that it was very dark, and behold, there appeared a smoking oven and a flaming torch which passed between these pieces. On that day the LORD made a covenant with Abram, saying, "To your descendants I have given this land, from the river of Egypt as far as the great river, the river Euphrates: the Kenite and the Kenizzite and the Kadmonite and the Hittite and the Perizzite and the Rephaim and the Amorite and the Canaanite and the Girgashite and the Jebusite" (Genesis 15:9-21).

Read back over this passage and then answer the following questions:

1. Who or what passed through the pieces of the animals?

2. What was Abraham doing?

3. What did God promise Abraham?

4. Where did the children of Israel live as slaves for four hundred years, then depart with many possessions?

5. Mark the word "covenant" and list below what you learn.

DAY FIVE

The Old Testament Hebrew word for covenant, *beyrith*, means a compact or agreement made by passing through pieces of flesh. To enter into a covenant was to enter into a solemn, binding agreement.

In Genesis 15:9-21, when God alone—and not Abraham—passed through the pieces in the image of a flaming torch and a smoking oven, He was signifying that this was a covenant which would not be broken. On that day, God swore by Himself that the land would be Israel's forever. This covenant was later confirmed to Isaac and Jacob.

In Exodus 2:24 when the sons of Israel sighed and cried out to God because of their bondage in Egypt, "God heard their groaning; and God remembered His covenant with Abraham, Isaac, and Jacob," and sent Moses to deliver them.

Because God is a covenant-keeping God, because He can neither lie nor alter the words which have gone forth from His mouth, Israel will always remain a nation. Because Habakkuk grasped this by faith, he knew that they would not die. God would chasten them as a nation, but He would not exterminate them as a people.

Even before the final Babylonian siege of Jerusalem, God sent word through a letter from Jeremiah to those in exile, giving them this promise: "'When seventy years have been completed for Babylon, I will visit you and fulfill My good word to you, to bring you back to this place. For I know the plans that I have for you,' declares the Lord, 'plans for welfare and not for calamity to give you a future and a hope'" (Jeremiah 29:10-11). God would keep His covenant.

Even though you might not understand why God allows bad things to happen to His people, do you think you can trust a covenant-keeping God? Will you stop right now and thank God that because you are His through the new covenant of grace, that the plans He has for *you* are plans for welfare and not for calamity, to give *you* a future and a hope? Your hope is heaven. Your future is eternal life. Choose to believe what He has promised.

Israel would not cease as a nation. God assured Jeremiah of this:

Thus says the LORD,
Who gives the sun for light by day,
And the fixed order of the moon
and the stars for light by night,
Who stirs up the sea so that its waves roar;
The LORD of hosts is His name:
"If this fixed order departs from before Me,"
declares the LORD,
"Then the offspring of Israel also shall cease
From being a nation before Me forever."
Thus says the LORD,
"If the heavens above can be measured,
And the foundations of the earth searched out
below, Then I will also cast off all the off-
spring of Israel for all that they have done,"
declares the LORD.

"Behold, days are coming," declares the LORD,
"when the city shall be rebuilt for the LORD
from the Tower of Hananel to the Corner Gate.
And the measuring line shall go out farther
straight ahead to the hill Gareb; then it will
turn to Goah. And the whole valley of the dead
bodies and of the ashes, and all the fields as far
as the brook Kidron, to the corner of the Horse
Gate toward the east, shall be holy to the LORD;
it shall not be plucked up, or overthrown anymore forever" (Jeremiah 31:35-40).

A day will come when Israel will never be overthrown or judged again. That day has not yet come,
but I believe it is on the horizon. Habakkuk talked
about it in the third chapter of his book when he told
of the Lord coming from Teman. And the apostle Paul
wrote about it in his letter to the Romans: "Thus all
Israel will be saved; just as it is written, 'THE DELIVERER
WILL COME FROM ZION, HE WILL REMOVE UNGODLINESS FROM
JACOB. AND THIS IS MY COVENANT WITH THEM, WHEN I TAKE
AWAY THEIR SINS.'. . . For the gifts and the calling of God
are irrevocable" (Romans 11:26-27,29).

Israel would be judged, but not die as a nation.

The history of Israel ought to give you great comfort, Beloved. For the existence of this nation, their return to the land of promise, and the blossoming of that land are all testimony to the fact that the promises of God are yea and amen whether given to Israel or given to the Church. God judged and scattered the Israelites among all the nations of the earth, yet they are still a separate and distinct people.

The people of Israel are now back in their land and recognized as a nation. Soon they shall recognize Jesus when they see Him come from Teman and go forth for the salvation of His people—His anointed (Habakkuk 3:3-13).

Let me say it again: Habakkuk knew that Israel would not die because he knew His God.

How well do you know your God, my friend? Note that I did not ask you what you know about His ways, but how well you know *Him.*

"The people who know their God will display strength and take action" (Daniel 11:32b).

DAY SIX

A friend of mine once suffered a total breakdown. Because of a certain sin she committed, she felt God could not forgive her. What a lie this is from the Enemy! When you sin as a child of God, God will discipline you, but He will never forsake you nor abandon you (Hebrews 13:5-6).God never casts off His own. How vital it is that you remember this truth.

We know that Habakkuk understood and rested in this truth, for he said, "We will not die" (Habakkuk 1:12).

Habakkuk knew God was a covenant-keeping God.

This same truth was also confirmed to Jeremiah:

> Thus says the LORD, "If you can break My
> covenant for the day, and My covenant for the
> night, so that day and night will not be at their
> appointed time, then My covenant may also be
> broken with David My servant that he shall not
> have a son to reign on his throne . . . .
>
> "If My covenant for day and night stand not,
> and the fixed patterns of heaven and earth I
> have not established, then I would reject the
> descendants of Jacob and David My servant,
> not taking from his descendants rulers over the
> descendants of Abraham, Isaac, and Jacob. But
> I will restore their fortunes and will have mercy
> on them" (Jeremiah 33:20-21,25-26).

If you are a believer, a true child of God, a new
creature in Christ Jesus, you are in covenant with Jesus
Christ. Do you remember what Jesus did on the night
that He was betrayed?

> And while they were eating, Jesus took some
> bread, and after a blessing, He broke it and
> gave it to the disciples, and said, "Take, eat;
> this is My body." And when He had taken a
> cup and given thanks, He gave it to them, say-
> ing, "Drink from it, all of you; for this is My
> blood of the covenant, which is poured out for
> many for forgiveness of sins. But I say to you, I
> will not drink of this fruit of the vine from now
> on until that day when I drink it new with you
> in My Father's kingdom" (Matthew 26:26-29).

Did you note that Jesus assured His disciples they
would drink the cup with Him once again "in My
Father's kingdom"? What was Jesus promising them?
He was saying, in essence, that the covenant into
which they were entering would guarantee them that

one day they would spend eternity together in the Father's kingdom.

Did this promise mean they would never sin again? No; it meant that because they believed in Him, they would have forgiveness of sins and eternal life. That was the covenant of grace. Not grace that would give them license to live in sin, but grace that would enable them by the gift of the Holy Spirit to overcome the law of sin and death. When they did sin, they were to confess their sins and God would be faithful and just to forgive their sins, and to cleanse them from all unrighteousness (1 John 1:9).

When you sin, God will have to discipline you, but He will never leave you nor forsake you, because He has made a covenant with you.

When God disciplines you, that doesn't mean He has forsaken you: Like Habakkuk, you must know you "will not die" (i.e., God will not cast you off forever). God is simply acting according to His character and fulfilling His purpose. "When we are judged, we are disciplined by the Lord in order that we may not be condemned along with the world" (1 Corinthians 11:32).

Going back to my friend who had the breakdown, how I would love to put my arms around her and tell her that God could *never* fail to forgive her. For Him not to forgive would be to go against His covenant! He loves her with an everlasting love, and, like Israel, the plans He has for her are plans for her welfare and her good, to give her a future and a hope.

DAY SEVEN

What Judah had sown, Judah would reap.

Among other things, Israel's sin had been destruction and violence (Habakkuk 1:2-3). Now God was bringing a destructive and violent people to judge them, a "fierce and impetuous people who march throughout the earth to seize dwelling places which are not theirs. They are dreaded and feared" (vv. 6-7).

Judah had turned from the Rock, the Fountain of Living Waters, to walk her own way, despising the Word of the Lord and refusing to hear what God was saying. Now Judah would be invaded by a people who walked the same way. God said of Judah's invaders:

> "Their justice and authority originate with
> themselves. . . .
> They fly like an eagle swooping down to
> devour.
> All of them come for violence.
> Their horde of faces moves forward.
> They collect captives like sand.
> They mock at kings,
> And rulers are a laughing matter to them.
> They laugh at every fortress,
> And heap up rubble to capture it"
> (Habakkuk 1:7,8-10).

Judgment was certain for Judah. God's people hadn't taken God at His Word. They hadn't believed He would do what He said He would do if they did not walk in the obedience of faith. What could Habakkuk do? He had walked uprightly, but he was in the minority. He was part of a remnant of righteous people who mourned over all that was happening, yet who lived in a wicked land that was about to be invaded.

How Habakkuk needed to remember that God was *the Rock!* When the storms of affliction came and the winds of violence blew against Judah, only those who had built their lives on the Rock would stand.

Habakkuk addresses God, "And Thou, O Rock, hast established them to correct" (1:12). From the time Moses struck the rock in the wilderness, causing water to flow freely, God had been known as the Rock.

Paul tells us in 1 Corinthians that when the children of Israel came out of Egypt they "all drank the same spiritual drink, for they were drinking from a spiritual rock which followed them; and the rock was Christ" (1 Corinthians 10:4).

Just before Moses died, he spoke in the hearing of all of the assembly of Israel the words of a song in which he made numerous references to God as our Rock. Take time to read that song in Deuteronomy 32:1-43. Note below all that you learn about your God, the Rock.

Now, how can you apply to your own life the insights you have gleaned today? Write out three sentences beginning with, "I learned . . . ," recording what you learned; then finish the sentence by adding, "therefore I . . . ," recording what you will do in light of what you learned.

Because we find ourselves living in the midst of a violent, destructive, sinful, unstable society, it is critical that we carefully build our lives on the Rock of Who

He is . . . and then learn to run to the Rock Who is higher than we are. If we will live in this manner, we will find ourselves able to live stable, consistent lives, unmoved by all the problems going on about us.

I am sure that David's writings were of great comfort to Habakkuk. How often the psalmist referred to God as his Rock! In fact, in David's last words he referred to God as the Rock of Israel (2 Samuel 23:3). Why? Because in his conflicts with Saul and his enemies, David ran to the Rock which was higher than he. Delivered again and again, he would sing:

> "The LORD is my rock and my fortress and my
>   deliverer; My God, my rock, in whom I take
>   refuge. . . .
> The LORD lives, and blessed be my rock;
> And exalted be God, the rock of my salvation,
> The God who executes vengeance for me,
> And brings down peoples under me,
> Who also brings me out from my enemies;
> Thou dost even lift me above
> those who rise up against me;
> Thou dost rescue me from the violent man.
> Therefore I will give thanks to Thee, O LORD,
> among the nations,
> And I will sing praises to Thy name.
> He is a tower of deliverance to His king,
> and shows lovingkindness to His anointed,
> To David and his descendants forever"
> (2 Samuel 22:2-3,47-51).

How I pray that you will be able to say with David, "He only is my rock and my salvation, my stronghold; I shall not be shaken. On God my salvation and my glory rest; the rock of my strength, my refuge is in God" (Psalm 62:6-7).

Notes

1. In Genesis 17, God changed Abram's name to Abraham.

Chapter 5

HE'S THERE,
THERE'S A PURPOSE
IN IT ALL

DAY ONE

How can you have a triumphant faith when life is so full of stress? How do you watch all that is taking place around you without falling apart?

It's all a matter of perspective.

Our second principle gives that perspective: **History centers on two peoples: the nation of Israel and the Church of Jesus Christ.** God is in charge of history; it is His story. And all that He does pivots on Israel or the Church.

When stressful times smash into our lives, we need to ask, "What is God doing in my life, in the Church, or in the nation of Israel?" All that happens will somehow relate to God's purpose for Israel or for His Church.

We see this truth in the book of Habakkuk. A whole nation had been raised up by God and given a place of world dominance simply to act as a rod of discipline. God "established them [the Babylonians] to correct" (Habakkuk 1:12).

Before the Babylonians were ever a world power, God said to Israel, "If you will diligently obey the LORD your God . . . the LORD your God will set you high above all the nations of the earth" (Deuteronomy 28:1).

With that promise, God spoke through Moses to tell them the blessings that would be theirs—including the promise that He would cause all of their enemies to be defeated before them!

Along with that promise of blessing, however, came the assurance of cursing for disobedience: "But it shall come about, if you will not obey the LORD your God, to observe to do all His commandments and His statutes with which I charge you today, that all these curses shall come upon you and overtake you" (Deuteronomy 28:15).

Take a few minutes and read Deuteronomy 28, noting the various kinds of blessings and curses. You might find it helpful to also record below the various categories into which these blessings and curses fall.

Among the curses you read is this: "The LORD will bring a nation against you from afar . . . a nation of fierce countenance who shall have no respect for the old, nor show favor to the young. Moreover, it shall eat the offspring of your herd and the produce of your ground until you are destroyed, who also leaves you no grain, new wine, or oil, nor the increase of your herd or the young of your flock" (Deuteronomy 28:49-51). God also told them that the enemy would lay siege against them, moving the Israelites to eat their own children! (Deuteronomy 28:53-57).

Awful, isn't it? Yet because they refused to obey, that is exactly what happened.

And how did Habakkuk handle the stress of it all? *He saw the bigger picture.* He knew that God would have to judge Israel, but he also knew that by faith he could live above the stress.

Beloved, you can do the same. Instead of being frustrated and overwhelmed by all that is going on in our world, go to the Lord and ask Him to give you His eternal perspective. Like Habakkuk, keep watch in the Word of God and allow Him to speak to you (Habakkuk 2:1). Live by what you know from God's Word rather than by your present experiences.

DAY TWO

Have you ever wrestled with why the wicked *seem* to prosper and why the righteous seem *not* to prosper?

Even after Habakkuk confirmed in his heart that God was from everlasting, his Creator, his Holy One, and his Rock, he was still troubled. How could his God allow such wicked and treacherous men like the Babylonians to be His instrument for judging the covenant nation? It was perplexing and disturbing. Was

God going to allow the Babylonians to "empty their net [of their catch of men] and continually slay nations without sparing"? (Habakkuk 1:17).

At this point Habakkuk had to get alone with God and wait for His answer. Can you relate to that? Are there times when life just doesn't seem right, fair, equitable? You ask yourself, *Does it really pay to be a Christian, to live a holy life?*

What you are going through is not unique. Habakkuk wrestled with it. So did Asaph. Asaph's wrestlings are recorded for us in Psalm 73, which is printed out below. Read it carefully, noting in the space that follows the things that troubled him.

PSALM 73

Surely God is good to Israel,
To those who are pure in heart!
But as for me, my feet came close to stumbling;
My steps had almost slipped.
For I was envious of the arrogant,
As I saw the prosperity of the wicked.
For there are no pains in their death;
And their body is fat.
They are not in trouble as other men;
Nor are they plagued like mankind.
Therefore pride is their necklace;
The garment of violence covers them.
Their eye bulges from fatness;
The imaginations of their heart run riot.
They mock, and wickedly speak of oppression;
They speak from on high.
They have set their mouth against the heavens,
And their tongue parades through the earth.

Therefore his people return to this place;
And waters of abundance are drunk by them.
And they say, "How does God know?
And is there knowledge with the Most High?"
Behold, these are the wicked;

And always at ease, they have increased in
wealth.
Surely in vain I have kept my heart pure,
And washed my hands in innocence;
For I have been stricken all day long,
And chastened every morning.

If I had said, "I will speak thus,"
Behold, I should have betrayed
the generation of Thy children.
When I pondered to understand this,
It was troublesome in my sight
Until I came into the sanctuary of God;
Then I perceived their end.
Surely Thou dost set them in slippery places;
Thou dost cast them down to destruction.
How they are destroyed in a moment!
They are utterly swept away by sudden terrors!
Like a dream when one awakes,
O Lord, when aroused, Thou wilt despise their
form.

When my heart was embittered,
And I was pierced within,
Then I was senseless and ignorant;
I was like a beast before Thee.
Nevertheless I am continually with Thee;
Thou hast taken hold of my right hand.
With Thy counsel Thou wilt guide me,
And afterward receive me to glory.

Whom have I in heaven but Thee?
And besides Thee, I desire nothing on earth.
My flesh and my heart may fail,
But God is the strength of my heart
and my portion forever.
For, behold, those who are far from Thee will
perish;
Thou hast destroyed all those who
are unfaithful to Thee.
But as for me, the nearness of God is my good;

> I have made the Lord GOD my refuge,
> That I may tell of all Thy works.

1. What, in particular, troubled Asaph?

2. What effect did this have on Asaph?

3. What gave Asaph the proper perspective?

4. What did you learn from Asaph's relationship with God that you can apply to your own life?

In Psalm 73, Asaph shared how his feet came close to stumbling, for he was envious of the arrogant as he saw their prosperity. They denied that God even knew what was going on. They were at ease, increasing in wealth, while Asaph suffered continually.

Asaph could not reason all of this out. Finally, he did as Habakkuk did. He went to God for His perspective. He had to get alone, go into the sanctuary of God and let God speak to him. Then Asaph, like Habakkuk, got a proper perspective on life.

Both saw the end of unrighteous men, the judgment of God upon the wicked. Then they understood that God was all that they needed. Habakkuk saw God as his strength, his enabler. Asaph wrote: "Whom have I in heaven but Thee? And besides Thee, I desire nothing on earth. My flesh and my heart may fail, but God is the strength of my heart and my portion forever. . . . the nearness of God is my good" (Psalm 73:25-26, 28).

This, Beloved, is what I want for you: *Time alone with God.*

In nearness to Him, you can get His perspective on life so you can know how to live. I pray you will take time to meditate on what you have studied so its truth becomes bone of your bone and flesh of your flesh.

DAY THREE

Parts of the world have suffered greatly because of adverse weather—there has been either too much water or not enough, too much heat or bitter cold.

I remember when a drought hit the United States a number of summers ago. Driving through Atlanta, I saw a sign in front of a business that read, Pray for Rain. I was impressed that someone realized where rain came from. Yet, as I thought about it, I felt we needed to go a step beyond praying for rain, and ask God why He had *withheld* the rain.

Could it be because of our sin? Was God trying to speak to America? To draw us to our knees in repentance? To remind us that it is "the LORD our God, Who gives rain in its season, both the autumn rain and the spring rain, Who keeps for us the appointed weeks of the harvest" (Jeremiah 5:24)?

Could it be we do not realize that what God said to Judah in Jeremiah 5:25-31 He could also be saying to us?

"Your iniquities have turned these away,
And your sins have withheld good from you.
For wicked men are found among My people,
They watch like fowlers lying in wait;
They set a trap,
They catch men.
Like a cage full of birds,
So their houses are full of deceit;
Therefore they have become great and rich.
They are fat, they are sleek,
They also excel in deeds of wickedness;
They do not plead the cause,
The cause of the orphan, that they may prosper;
And they do not defend the rights of the poor.
Shall I not punish these people?" declares the
    LORD,
"On a nation such as this
Shall I not avenge Myself?

"An appalling and horrible thing
Has happened in the land:
The prophets prophesy falsely,
And the priests rule on their own authority;
And My people love it so!"

All of history—including the famines, droughts, plagues, and economic disasters—centers on what God wants to bring to pass regarding either Israel or the Church. Sometimes we forget that God is moving throughout the nations of the earth, calling out a people for Himself. He uses all sorts of means to bring them to their knees so that they might see that He is the Lord God and that they need to worship Him and submit to the Lordship of His Son. Whatever means He uses, it is worth it if it causes us to pass from death to life by believing on His Son. "Or do you think lightly of the riches of His kindness and forbearance and patience, not knowing that the kindness of God leads you to repentance?" (Romans 2:4).

Your whole perspective on current events can change if you know that the God Who is in charge of history is working everything according to His purpose for Israel and for the Church—not only for those who have already heard His voice, but for those who have yet to believe.

Take a few minutes, Beloved, to think of what's happening in our world, our society. Do you think God is trying to get our attention? How? Write it down in the space below.

Now, how do you think God would have you pray?

DAY FOUR

There is a purpose in what God does.

This is the third principle we need to consider. Whether we understand or not, our God is working, and He knows what He is doing! *What He is doing will always work together for the good of the individual Christian, the Church, and the nation of Israel.*

When Habakkuk unloaded his burden on God, asking Him why He hadn't heard his cry for help and why He allowed all of the wickedness that he saw, God assured Habakkuk He was working. Read Habakkuk 1:5 again: "Look among the nations! Observe! Be astonished! Wonder! Because I am doing something in your days you would not believe if you were told."

Habakkuk didn't know or understand it. And as a matter of fact, Habakkuk would have had a hard time even believing it. But God was working! God was carrying out His plan and His purpose in history.

Isaiah 14:24 and 27 are such comforting and pertinent verses that I want to remind you of them again. Meditate on them: "The LORD of hosts has sworn saying, 'Surely, just as I have intended so it has happened, and just as I have planned so it will stand.' . . . For the LORD of hosts has planned, and who can frustrate it? And as for His stretched-out hand, who can turn it back?"

Oh, Beloved, do you see it? From the destiny of the nations to the destiny of your life, *God is in control.* He has a plan, and that plan is according to His purpose in your life. His purpose is to make you into the image of His Son, the Lord Jesus Christ. Nothing can frustrate or abort God's plans, either for Israel, the Church, the nations, or you.

Stop and think about it. Like Habakkuk, you may not think God is working, but He is. Believe Him, and you will have an overcoming faith.

Read and meditate on Romans 8:37-39:

But in all these things we overwhelmingly conquer through Him who loved us. For I am convinced that neither death, nor life, nor angels, nor principalities, nor things present, nor things to come, nor powers, nor height, nor depth, nor any other created thing, shall be able to separate us from the love of God, which is in Christ Jesus our Lord.

Day Five

God is at work and He always acts in accordance with His character.

Sometimes we shipwreck our faith by thinking that God is like man. We begin to evaluate His actions on the basis of how *we* would behave if we were God. We judge God from man's perspective.

For instance, when we hear of disasters in which thousands are killed and say, "But a loving God wouldn't do that," we evaluate His actions according to our concept of love. Or, we fail to look at the sum total of God's attributes. We isolate some of them, forgetting that what God does is always and totally consistent with Who He is.

We tend to evaluate everything from the realm of our experiences with other human beings. We measure God by how others think, respond, react, perform, or love. Then, if we don't know the Word of God or if we do not stop to consider and believe what it says, we think that God is going to act—or *ought* to act—in the same way as man.

We forget God's ways are not our ways, nor His thoughts our thoughts.

"For My thoughts are not your thoughts,
Neither are your ways My ways," declares the
    LORD. "For as the heavens are higher than
    the earth,
So are My ways higher than your ways,
And My thoughts than your thoughts"
(Isaiah 55:8-9).

In other words, *He is God*. Transcendent. Holy.
Incomprehensible.

We cannot sit in judgment or evaluate God and His
actions, because we are finite. We are limited in our
thinking, in our experience, in our ability, and in the
brevity of our lives.

Consider part of God's reply to Job:

"Now gird up your loins like a man;
I will ask you, and you instruct Me.
Will you really annul My judgment?
Will you condemn Me that you may be
    justified?
Or do you have an arm like God,
And can you thunder with a voice like His?"
(Job 40:7-9).

Remember: God will always act according to *His*
character, not man's. He can never divorce Himself
from Who He is, nor can He act contrary to His character. "If we are faithless, He remains faithful; for He
cannot deny Himself" (2 Timothy 2:13).

Because of this glorious truth, dear child of God,
you can know with absolute certainty that while
nothing else may be consistent in your life, God is.
He is immutable; He does not change.

List on the next page anything that has caused you
to question or doubt God. Be honest about disappoint-
ments you have felt in His dealings with you or others.
Next to each item, write out what attribute of God this
causes you to question.

DAY SIX

Habakkuk cried out to God because God didn't seem to be doing anything about the violence, destruction, and injustice taking place in Judah. Yet when Habakkuk brought this burden to God, He assured Habakkuk that He *was* doing something. God had raised up the Babylonians, who would be His instrument of judgment against the sins of Judah.

But this wasn't what Habakkuk expected!

How could God use a wicked people like the idolatrous Babylonians to swallow up a people more righteous than they? (Habakkuk 1:13). Even though the distressed prophet rehearsed what he knew about God, calling Him the Holy One, the Rock, and remembering that God was a covenant-keeping God, he *still* had trouble.

How could a holy God, Whose eyes were "too pure to approve evil" and Who could "not look on wickedness with favor" allow a nation like Babylon to triumph over them? (1:13).

When God judges us, He can use anyone He pleases. The Bible tells us that "the LORD has made everything for its own purpose, even the wicked for the day of evil" (Proverbs 16:4).

God never told Habakkuk why He was using the Babylonians, but simply that He was. And please note that He did not scold nor chastise Habakkuk for asking. Isn't this wonderful? God is approachable. You can ask Him anything. It is so much better to verbalize what is on your heart and to communicate openly with Him rather than allow it to fester inside. A wise child will bring all of his doubts and perplexities to his heavenly Father. Be wise, Beloved.

As Habakkuk waited to hear how God would answer, God eventually let him know that judgment was coming. It was certain. And here we learn again that God, because He is God, must move accordingly.

God calls His people to be holy, even as He is holy. "As obedient children, do not be conformed to the former lusts which were yours in your ignorance, but like the Holy One who called you, be holy yourselves also in all your behavior; because it is written, 'YOU SHALL BE HOLY, FOR I AM HOLY'" (1 Peter 1:14-16).

When we are disobedient, God in His holiness cannot approve our evil nor look upon our wickedness with favor. Rather, He must judge it. His character demands it. In 1 Peter 4:17 we read, "For it is time for judgment to begin with the household of God; and if it begins with us first, what will be the outcome for those who do not obey the gospel of God?"

When a holy God judges His people, it is always to discipline. To let sin go on and on, unchecked, would only encourage us to sin more.

God warns us through His prophets and His Word. But when we continually refuse to believe the message of His prophets, God must move in judgment. And He acts in this manner because He must remain faithful to Who He is and to His covenant with His people.

Many times you will see the word *Selah* used in the Psalms, just as it is used in Habakkuk 3. Scholars believe *Selah* means "pause and think on these things." Therefore, my friend, I want to close your day and mine with *Selah*.

DAY SEVEN

Many Christians have waged war on their knees against evil rulers and nations, only to see the malicious conquests continue.

Where was God? Why wasn't He hearing their prayers?

Would these Hitlers of history continue unchecked forever as they sought to annihilate the chosen of God, Jews and Gentiles?

How can a righteous and holy God allow "the wicked [to] swallow up those more righteous than they"? (Habakkuk 1:13). Habakkuk could understand how God had to judge Judah, but why would He allow these evil men to treat those whom they conquered with as little value as fish in the sea, dragging them away with their net, slaying them without sparing? Would God never stop them, never bring their wickedness to a halt? (Habakkuk 1:14-17).

Have you ever felt the same way? Have you ever felt like your prayers were useless because the actions of wicked men continued unchecked? Did you want to give up? Quit praying? Walk away and forget it all? When you find yourself unable to understand the ways of God, or when you find yourself frustrated because God does not seem to be hearing, you must learn a lesson from Habakkuk. Listen to what he did:

I will stand on my guard post
And station myself on the rampart;

> And I will keep watch to see what He will
>   speak to me,
> And how I may reply when I am reproved
>   (Habakkuk 2:1).

Habakkuk didn't quit. Habakkuk *waited* . . . with a listening ear. Despair walks away, thinking God doesn't care. Faith waits and listens, knowing that in God's perfect time He will speak. Silence does not mean that God has abandoned you, or that He does not care. It doesn't mean that God is like man, showing anger by refusing to communicate. When God is silent, it simply means that at this point He has, for some reason, not yet chosen to say anymore. Yet, in the silence He is still fulfilling His purpose; He is still acting according to His character and sovereignty—whether we understand or not.

Waiting is hard. Silence is even harder. And yet, Beloved, if you and I will only remember that although the wicked seemingly go unchecked, God is in control. He is in charge of history. Therefore, whatever is happening will somehow work out for the good of Israel or the Church.

There is a purpose in what God is doing. When He is ready to tell us, He will. Until then, like Habakkuk, we need to keep the watch of faith, to see what God will say to us.

When He does speak, what are you to do?

Chapter 6

HE'S THERE,
DON'T BE ASHAMED;
PROCLAIM HIS WORD

DAY ONE

Although Habakkuk questioned God, he didn't walk away. He waited to hear what God had to say. He was not disappointed; God spoke. And Habakkuk learned some wonderful lessons, received a commission, and wrote it all down for us in a book!

If you, too, will learn to wait upon God, to get alone with Him, and remain silent so that you can hear His voice when He is ready to speak to you, what a difference it will make in your life! I think many of our problems overwhelm us simply because we do not set

aside the time to be alone with God. I don't see how
any Christian can survive, let alone live life as more than
a conqueror, apart from a quiet time alone with God.

There are so many voices clamoring for our attention. There are so many philosophies and ideologies
thrown at us through our educational systems and the
numerous books in print. The radio, the television, or
the stereo blares incessantly in many homes throughout the day and night.

If we do not shut it all off and get alone with Him,
how can we hear the still, small voice of God? "And
after the earthquake a fire; but the LORD was not in the
fire; and after the fire a still small voice" (1 Kings
19:12, KJV).

God is no respecter of persons. "God is not one to
show partiality" (Acts 10:34). He will meet with us as
He met with Habakkuk, if we will get alone and wait
to hear what He says. "Wait for the LORD; be strong,
and let your heart take courage; yes, wait for the LORD"
(Psalm 27:14).

Luke 10:38-42 shows a contrast in two lives. Read
it carefully. When you finish, make a list of everything
you learn about Mary and about Martha.

LUKE 10:38-42

Now as they were traveling along, He entered a
certain village; and a woman named Martha
welcomed Him into her home. And she had a
sister called Mary, who moreover was listening
to the Lord's word, seated at His feet. But
Martha was distracted with all her preparations;
and she came up to Him, and said, "Lord, do
You not care that my sister has left me to do all
the serving alone? Then tell her to help me."
But the Lord answered and said to her, "Martha,
Martha, you are worried and bothered about so
many things; but only a few things are necessary,

really only one, for Mary has chosen the good part, which shall not be taken away from her."

What have you learned about Mary and Martha?

Mary:

Martha:

What does Jesus say is the one thing that is needful? How do you get it? What did Mary do? Write out your answer . . . and then go and do likewise.

DAY TWO

To hear God's Word is to become accountable to it.

That is an awesome fact, one that you may not want to believe. But it is true. It does not matter whether you believe what God says or not, or even *like* what He says. You and I are accountable simply because God has spoken. It is as true for you and me as it was true for Habakkuk.

Apparently Habakkuk did not have to wait long before God replied to his questions. Listen to what God said:

"Record the vision
And inscribe it on tablets,
That the one who reads it may run.
For the vision is yet for the appointed time;
It hastens toward the goal, and it will not fail.
Though it tarries, wait for it;
For it will certainly come, it will not delay"
(Habakkuk 2:2-3).

Whatever God says will come to pass *will* come to pass. Like it or not, want it or not, it is certain, because God is certain. It may be a long time before it happens. It may even be centuries or a millennium or two. But if God says something will occur, then it will, because as He has "planned so it will stand" (Isaiah 14:24).

Habakkuk was to record the vision on a tablet so that others could read it. Eventually, you and I would read it. Theologians believe it was probably engraved on large clay tablets which would be displayed in a public place such as the temple—or maybe even in the market-place or city square. There it could be read by all.

In this case, the reading of it placed a responsibility upon the readers: they were to run and proclaim it.

It's always a delight to spread good news. Some people take pleasure in spreading bad news about others. Few, however, delight to speak the news of God's judgment, especially if it not only pertains to others but to their own people—or even themselves! Why? Because no one wants to hear bad news. As a matter of fact, when people hear bad news, they often tend to discredit both the message and the messenger.

When the Old Testament prophets spoke of God's impending judgment, the people often tried to get rid of them. They did this to Jeremiah. They loved the false prophets and their message of "peace, peace," even though it was a lie. But they didn't want to hear God's message: Repent or be judged.

Want it or not, the people were to hear it. Read Jeremiah 1 in the paragraphs that follow:

JEREMIAH 1

The words of Jeremiah, the son of Hilkiah, of the priests who were in Anathoth in the land of Benjamin, to whom the word of the LORD came in the days of Josiah, the son of Amon, king of Judah, in the thirteenth year of his reign. It came also in the days of Jehoiakim, the son of Josiah, king of Judah, until the end of the eleventh year of Zedekiah, the son of Josiah, king of Judah, until the exile of Jerusalem in the fifth month.

Now the word of the LORD came to me saying,
"Before I formed you in the womb I knew you,
And before you were born I consecrated you;
I have appointed you a prophet to the nations."
Then I said, "Alas, Lord GOD!
Behold, I do not know how to speak,
Because I am a youth."
But the LORD said to me,
"Do not say, 'I am a youth,'
Because everywhere I send you, you shall go,
And all that I command you, you shall speak.
Do not be afraid of them,
For I am with you to deliver you," declares the
    LORD.
Then the LORD stretched out His hand and
    touched my mouth, and the LORD said to me,
"Behold, I have put My words in your mouth.
See, I have appointed you this day over the
    nations

and over the kingdoms,
To pluck up and to break down,
To destroy and to overthrow,
To build and to plant."

And the word of the LORD came to me saying, "What do you see, Jeremiah?" And I said, "I see a rod of an almond tree."

Then the LORD said to me, "You have seen well, for I am watching over My word to perform it."

And the word of the LORD came to me a second time saying, "What do you see?" And I said, "I see a boiling pot, facing away from the north." Then the LORD said to me, "Out of the north the evil will break forth on all the inhabitants of the land. For, behold, I am calling all the families of the kingdoms of the north," declares the LORD; "and they will come, and they will set each one his throne at the entrance of the gates of Jerusalem, and against all its walls round about, and against all the cities of Judah. And I will pronounce My judgments on them concerning all their wickedness, whereby they have forsaken Me and have offered sacrifices to other gods, and worshiped the works of their own hands. Now, gird up your loins, and arise, and speak to them all which I command you. Do not be dismayed before them, lest I dismay you before them. Now behold, I have made you today as a fortified city, and as a pillar of iron and as walls of bronze against the whole land, to the kings of Judah, to its princes, to its priests and to the people of the land. And they will fight against you, but they will not overcome you, for I am with you to deliver you," declares the LORD.

Answer the following questions. Read all of them before you begin, because some of your answers could apply to more than one question.

1. What specifically did God call Jeremiah to do, and where or to whom was he to go?

2. What judgments would God pronounce through Jeremiah and why?

3. What kind of a response could Jeremiah expect? How would he be received? What was Jeremiah to do in the light of it?

4. What could Jeremiah expect from God? Under what conditions, if any?

Remember, Jeremiah was Habakkuk's contemporary. They were both prophets sent to the southern kingdom to warn them of the impending Babylonian invasion.

Suppose God were to tell you to warn people to flee from His coming judgment. Would you? And what if they didn't want to listen? What if they gave you a hard time? What would you do?

DAY THREE

Will you have bloody hands, my friend, when you stand before your God?

When Paul told the elders at Ephesus, "I am innocent of the blood of all men. For I did not shrink from declaring to you the whole purpose of God" (Acts 20:26-27), what did he mean?

Paul was using a term used in Ezekiel chapters 3 and 33. As I shared in the first week of our study, Ezekiel was taken by the Babylonians in the second siege of Jerusalem. His prophecy was written from captivity.

I want us to take the next two days to look at the second and third chapters of Ezekiel, for I believe that what you see in these chapters will help you understand the gravity of knowing and proclaiming God's Word, whether people want to hear it or not.

Read through Ezekiel 2:1-3:11 and then answer the questions that follow this passage of Scripture.

EZEKIEL 2:1-3:11

Then He said to me, "Son of man, stand on your feet that I may speak with you!" And as He spoke to me the Spirit entered me and set me on my feet; and I heard Him speaking to me. Then He said to me, "Son of man, I am sending you to the sons of Israel, to a rebellious people who have rebelled against Me; they and their fathers have transgressed against Me to this very day. And I am sending you to them who are stubborn and obstinate children; and you shall say to them, 'Thus says the Lord GOD.' As for them, whether they listen or not—for they are a rebellious house—they will know that a prophet has been among them. And you, son of man, neither fear them nor fear their words, though thistles and thorns are with you and you sit on scorpions; neither fear their words nor be dismayed at their presence, for they are a rebellious house. But you shall speak My words to them whether they listen or not, for they are rebellious.

Now you, son of man, listen to what I am speaking to you; do not be rebellious like that rebellious house. Open your mouth and eat what I am giving you." Then I looked, behold, a hand was extended to me; and lo, a scroll was in it. When He spread it out before me, it was written on the front and back; and written on it were lamentations, mourning and woe.

Then He said to me, "Son of man, eat what you find; eat this scroll, and go, speak to the house of Israel." So I opened my mouth, and He fed me this scroll. And He said to me, "Son of man, feed your stomach, and fill your body with this scroll which I am giving you." Then I ate it, and it was sweet as honey in my mouth.

Then He said to me, "Son of man, go to the house of Israel and speak with My words to them. For you are not being sent to a people of unintelligible speech or difficult language, but to the house of Israel, nor to many peoples of unintelligible speech or difficult language, whose words you cannot understand. But I have sent you to them who should listen to you; yet the house of Israel will not be willing to listen to you, since they are not willing to listen to Me. Surely the whole house of Israel is stubborn and obstinate. Behold, I have made your face as hard as their faces, and your forehead as hard as their foreheads. Like emery harder than flint I have made your forehead. Do not be afraid of them or be dismayed before them, though they are a rebellious house." Moreover, He said to me, "Son of man, take into your heart all My words which I shall speak to you, and listen closely. And go to the exiles, to the sons of your people, and speak to them and tell them, whether they listen or not, 'Thus says the Lord GOD."

1. How does God describe the sons of Israel in this passage? What are they like? What have they done?

2. What was Ezekiel given to eat? Describe it from the text of Scripture which you just read.

3. What was Ezekiel to do in respect to the sons of Israel? How would they respond to them?

4. What was to be Ezekiel's response to them?

5. Do you see any parallels or application to your life? Look up Romans 15:4, then answer the question.

DAY FOUR

"Son of man, I have appointed you a watchman to the house of Israel; whenever you hear a word from My mouth, warn them from Me. When I say to the wicked, 'You shall surely die'; and you do not warn him or speak out to warn the wicked from his wicked way that he may live, that wicked man shall die in his iniquity, but his blood I will require at your hand. Yet if you have warned the wicked, and he does not turn from his wickedness or from his wicked way, he shall die in his iniquity; but you have delivered yourself. Again, when a righteous man turns away from his righteousness and commits iniquity, and I place an obstacle before him, he shall die; since you have not warned him, he shall die in his sin, and his righteous deeds which he has done shall not be remembered; but his blood I will require at your hand" (Ezekiel 3:17-20).

1. What was Ezekiel to do in respect to the wicked? Be specific in your answer.

2. What would happen to Ezekiel and to the wicked if Ezekiel did not do as he was told?

3. What would happen to the wicked if they did not listen?

Now, Beloved, what do you think Paul meant when he said he was guilty of the blood of no man (Acts 20:26-27)?

What will your hands be like when you stand before the Lord?

DAY FIVE

When the Lord answered Habakkuk, He showed him what was to come in the future. It was yet for an appointed time. God assured Habakkuk that although he would have to wait, it would not fail; it would come. It would not be late, according to God's timetable. At this point, you may wonder why I am stressing this. Let me explain.

God was giving Habakkuk a glimpse of the future—just as He has given us a glimpse, through His Word, of what is yet to come. The Word of God clearly states over and over that Jesus Christ is coming to the earth "a second time . . . to those who eagerly await Him" (Hebrews 9:28). And when He comes to earth the second time, He will thoroughly deal with all of the ungodly.

Listen to what God spoke through the apostle Paul: "For after all it is only just for God to repay with affliction those who afflict you, and to give relief to you who are afflicted and to us as well when the Lord Jesus shall be revealed from heaven with His mighty angels in flaming fire, dealing out retribution to those who do not know God and to those who do not obey the gospel of our Lord Jesus" (2 Thessalonians 1:6-8).

What you and I know of His coming and judgment of the wicked, we are to proclaim and to live in the light of—just as Habakkuk did. We are responsible to read the Word of God which is so accessible, and then run to proclaim it. We need to explain what we are learning in Habakkuk. We need to share that although God is seemingly allowing the wicked to prosper and destruction and violence to parade like conquerors through the cities of our land while justice is not upheld, there will come a day of reckoning. If men do not turn from their iniquity, they will experience the fierce wrath of Almighty God.

"Let the redeemed of the LORD say so" (Psalm 107:2). Selah.

DAY SIX

"History fails to record a single precedent in which nations subject to moral decay have not passed into political and economic decline. There has been either a spiritual awakening to overcome the moral collapse or a progressive deterioration leading to ultimate national disaster." [1]

America has never been worse off morally.

As recently as 1936, it was illegal for men to wear topless bathing suits in New York. U.S. men won topless rights after a decade of controversy. In the 30's, male bathers began discarding the shoulders-to-thighs tank suits for new swimming trunks.

In 1934, eight men were fined $1 each for topless bathing at Coney Island. "All of you fellows may be Adonises," said the presiding magistrate, a woman, "but there are many people who object to seeing so much of the human body exposed." A year later, a mass arrest of 42 topless males in Atlantic City, N.J., fattened the municipal coffers by $84. The city fathers declared: "We'll have no gorillas on our beaches."

Gradually, the guardians of national decency relented, and local ordinances were revised to allow topless bathing for men. In 1936, it was economy rather than morality that finally induced the Westchester, N.Y., County Park Commission to allow swimming trunks. The commission, which purchased suits for rental at county beaches and pools, found that the trunks were substantially cheaper." [2]

Now you can see total nudity not only on the beaches but also on cable TV in the United States and national television in some countries. And what about store magazine racks?

Billions of dollars are spent every year for pornographic materials. Overwhelming evidence shows that pornographic material inspires most sex crimes, especially the molesting of young children. And yet, instead of bringing swift judgment on the industry, it is imported into our schools in the name of health and sex education. I recently saw the series "Life Horizons" being used this way in Georgia schools. It shows graphic pictures of two young people having intercourse, with a close-up shot of the most intimate details. I was horrified and sick. I saw something I had never seen before and never needed to see. Nor did the children who saw it. It could only awaken curiosity and desire. No wonder the most endangered group of potential AIDS victims is our teenagers.

How did these things come to be allowed? Why hasn't our nation done something about it?

Do you think a holy God Whose name is *El Roi*, "the God Who sees," is going to let this pass unjudged? Proclaim it!

In the early years of television, Ozzie and Harriet slept in twin beds. By law, no television show was allowed to show a bedroom scene where a man and woman would be in the same bed—even though the actors were playing the roles of husband and wife.

Now television programs commonly show men and women—who aren't even married—in the same bed making love. Sometimes even two men are shown in bed together.

Do you think a holy God Whose name is *Jehovah Tsidkenu*, "the Lord our righteousness," is going to allow a nation that allows this behavior and promotes it—without blushing—to go unjudged? Proclaim it!

I remember that not too long ago any doctor caught performing an abortion would lose his license to practice medicine and could go to prison.

Do you think our Creator, *Elohim*, Who formed us in our mother's womb when we were made in secret, Whose eyes saw our unformed substance, is going to deem those innocent who consented to or performed these abortions? PROCLAIM IT!

It used to be a felony to practice homosexuality. Now the Gay Lobby is so brazen, and powerful that, for the first time in history, a plague, AIDS, has been treated as a political issue instead of a deadly health threat. An estimated 70 percent of all homosexuals in this nation are infected with the AIDS virus, yet instead of isolating them and bringing this plague to a halt, we protect them at the jeopardy of the nation. AIDS is fatal, and no cure is expected in this century.

"If the Gay Lobby has its way, this disease-ridden behavior could cause the collapse of the Western civilization," stated Congressman William E. Dannemeyer of California. The homosexual community *knows* what causes AIDS, and yet, will they stop? No; they simply become angry and belligerent because the government isn't spending enough to find a cure for a disease they wouldn't have to be exposed to if they would obey God's Word. When homosexuality or any sexual sin named in Leviticus 20 is not judged, it pollutes the land. Proclaim it!

And the LORD said, "The outcry of Sodom and Gomorrah is indeed great, and their sin is exceedingly grave. I will go down now, and see if they have done entirely according to its outcry, which has come to Me; and if not, I will know."

Then the men turned away from there and went toward Sodom, while Abraham was still standing before the LORD. And Abraham came near and said, "Wilt Thou indeed sweep away the righteous with the wicked? Suppose there are fifty righteous within the city; wilt Thou indeed sweep it away and not spare the place for the sake of the fifty righteous who are in it? Far be it from Thee to do such a thing, to slay the righteous with the wicked, so that the righteous and the wicked are treated alike. Far be it from Thee! Shall not the Judge of all the earth deal justly?". . . Then he said, "Oh may the LORD not be angry, and I shall speak only this once; suppose ten are found there?"

And [God] said, "I will not destroy it on account of the ten." And as soon as He had finished speaking to Abraham the LORD departed; and Abraham returned to his place (Genesis 18:20-25,32-33).

Genesis 19:24 tells us what happened later: "Then the LORD rained on Sodom and Gomorrah brimstone and fire from the LORD out of heaven."

Proclaim it! Proclaim it, lest their blood be on your hands.

Now, let me close with this question: How are we to proclaim His sure and just judgment? Think about it. Ask the Lord to show you ways that His coming judgment can be proclaimed to the world through your life, your speech, and your actions. List them below. Be specific.

"I was ticked off by your message and I want you to know it."

That's an encouraging message for a speaker! My feelings were somewhat assuaged, however, when I heard this woman's reason.

She didn't agree with my stand on immorality.

She believed sex was fine outside marriage—even if you were married—as long as your partner consented! As a matter of fact, if she wanted to have sex with others, according to her there was nothing in the Word of God against it—as long as there was mutual consent. She told me I simply didn't understand the true meaning of adultery and fornication.

Beside all that, she didn't like my reference to having a religion without a relationship to God. And all of that "born again talk" nauseated her!

The conversation went on for a while. Although she came on like gangbusters, I was excited. God had set a lost sheep right in my path in a one-on-one encounter. The thief was out to steal, kill, and destroy, but I knew the Shepherd wanted to say, "Here, sheepy, sheepy."

God's love welled up in my heart. I understood her rationalization of sin—I once sat where she sat. But now I was silently praying, listening, and waiting.

Then I felt the timing was of the Spirit. I leaned over to her and said, "You are going to want to slug me, and I understand, but I have to be honest with you. My friend, you and I don't have the same Father. You're in darkness. You're deceived. You have a religion and not a relationship. Your father is the devil. You're going to hell."

I didn't have to duck, although I was prepared to!

A day and a half later we had another conversation that lasted five hours. We talked until seven in the morning! This woman had come to blast one last word at me. Or so she thought. Our sovereign God had something else in mind. As she continued to argue her beliefs on morality and the Word, I simply took her to one Scripture after another, having her read it aloud. What was inscribed in God's Word, I proclaimed. Nothing else. Every time she wanted to argue, I simply said, "What does God say? Read it. Don't argue with me. He wrote it." All the while, I groaned inwardly in prayer, asking God to open blind eyes and turn this dear soul from darkness to light.

Finally I said, "Why don't you get on your knees and tell God what you think about what you have read. Argue with *Him*." We got on our knees. Her words turned to sobs, heaving out her sin. Suddenly she looked at me and said, "I feel so wicked, so desperately, desperately wicked. So despicable."

With tears in my eyes, I gently replied, "You are. You are desperately wicked. And what you have done is absolutely despicable. Tell God."

Well, what she hated happened—she was born again. Gloriously, wonderfully born again. Saved from the deepest of pits, from the cesspool of iniquity. As I sat there watching God be God, standing in awe of the new creation He had just brought into existence, over and over again I could hear in my heart Steve Green singing, "I have seen God's glory, I have lived and walked with Christ my Lord . . . ." And I had.

I tell you all this, Beloved, because of something this woman said to me: "I need to talk to someone strong who will meet me on my level. Someone I can sort out the garbage with. Someone who will handle me like you did—who'll not back down, who'll understand, not run away in disgust, and yet say it in such love."

Years ago, as I watched my friend Elizabeth McDonald, I learned how to speak the truth in love, how to lovingly confront people with God's impending judgment. Then as I matured in the Word, I saw what I had learned confirmed in the lives of Isaiah, Jeremiah, Ezekiel, and the other prophets. True prophets of God, those who serve as His spokesmen, do not dilute or alter His message. They're not dismayed by others' faces. They warn of the just judgment of God, but they do it in love, in tears.

I grieve when I hear what I believe to be erroneous teaching that says, in essence, "Prophets are just straightforward and hard. That's their personality." A believer's personality is to be controlled by Christ. No matter our gifts or our calling, we are to be filled with His Spirit, manifesting His love, grace, and mercy along with His holiness, righteousness, and just judgment.

Therefore, O watchman on the wall, when you seek to be guilty of the blood of no man as you read and proclaim God's Word, remember the truths of the following verses. Look them up, then record what you learn from observing what they say.

1. Galatians 5:22-26

2. 1 Corinthians 13:1-8

Chapter 7

HE'S THERE,
YOU CAN LIVE
BY FAITH

DAY ONE

After Habakkuk spilled out the questions of his heart, he did a very wise thing. He stood on his guard post, stationing himself on the rampart, and waited to see what God would say to him (Habakkuk 2:1).

It was then, in the silence, in the expectant waiting, that God spoke:

Then the LORD answered me and said,
"Record the vision

And inscribe it on tablets,
That the one who reads it may run.
For the vision is yet for the appointed time;
It hastens toward the goal, and it will not fail.
Though it tarries, wait for it;
For it will certainly come, it will not delay.
Behold, as for the proud one,
His soul is not right within him;
But the righteous will live by his faith"
(Habakkuk 2:2-4).

To Habakkuk, God gave the key, the key of all of life, the key to the whole Word of God: The righteous, the just, will live by faith.

I want to show you why I, along with others, believe that Habakkuk 2:4 is the key verse of the entire Bible. It will take a few days, but let's begin by looking at faith.

What does the Word of God mean when it speaks of faith? Faith is simply taking God at His Word. It is believing God. It is believing all that He says whether you understand it or not, whether you can explain it or not.

It is taking God at His Word. No matter how you feel, no matter how you read the circumstances, no matter what anyone else tells you about the truthfulness of what God says. God *is* truthful.

He does not lie. He cannot lie. Therefore, all that He says is truth. If anything or anyone contradicts the veracity of what God says, they are wrong. God's Word is truth. For that reason, the very plumbline of our faith is the Bible, the unadulterated Word of God.

When the Word of God talks about faith, it means more than intellectual assent. The Greek word for faith is *pistis,* and it means "a firm persuasion, a conviction based on hearing."[1] The word for believe is *pisteuo,* and it means "to be persuaded of, to place confidence in."[2] Biblical belief, then, signifies not mere credence of, but reliance upon all that God says.

As you study God's Word, you see basically three elements involved in true faith or belief. They are (1) a firm conviction that fully acknowledges what God has revealed, (2) a surrender to what God has revealed, and (3) conduct that is produced as a result of a personal surrender to what God has revealed.

The author of the book of Hebrews defines faith in this way: "Now faith is the assurance of things hoped for, the conviction of things not seen" (Hebrews 11:1). Under divine inspiration, the author of Hebrews also gives us insight into a critical truth upon which all of man's life and future pivot: "Without faith it is impossible to please Him, for he who comes to God must believe that He is, and that He is a rewarder of those who seek Him" (Hebrews 11:6). Therefore, if the just shall live by faith, the just must believe what God says, surrender to it, and live accordingly. Otherwise, they cannot please God.

Do you *believe* that the Bible is the inerrant, verbally-inspired Word of God? (Note that I emphasized *believe*.) Write out your answer to that question.

If so, then how are you going to live?

If you don't believe the Bible is inerrant and verbally inspired, explain why.

If pure, unadulterated truth cannot be found in the Bible, then where will you find it?

If you have an International Inductive Study Bible, there is an article in the front that explains the origins of the Bible and how we know it's the Word of God. You'll want to read that; it's quite enlightening.

DAY TWO

Yesterday we defined faith. Today we want to see where faith comes from.

Romans 10:17 says, "So faith comes from hearing, and hearing by the word of Christ."

Faith is a firm persuasion, a conviction based on hearing. Therefore, according to Romans 10:17, faith comes from hearing God's Word.

The Bible is God's Word to man. It is God-breathed and God-preserved from the time that Moses, under the moving of God's Spirit, began to write the Pentateuch—to the time the apostle John completed the Scripture by writing in Revelation the things which were, which are, and which are yet to come.

When Jesus came to earth as the Son of Man, He never contradicted the Scriptures, nor did He ever imply they were inaccurate in any detail. What modern scholars have deemed mere stories recorded by man in order to illustrate a point, Jesus considered historical occurrences—events that actually took place.

Look up the following verses about events which some would tell you are myths, and record what you learn from the text regarding these events.

1. Creation—Matthew 19:4-6

2. A universal flood in the days of Noah—Matthew 24:37-39 and 2 Peter 3:1-7

3. Jonah in the belly of a great fish—Matthew 12:38-41

Oh, my friend, never let anyone tell you God's Word contains errors. Will you not believe the sovereign, omnipotent, omniscient God? Will you not believe His Son, Who is one with the Father and called "The Truth"? Or will you believe men tutored by men over and against the testimony of the One Who, as the Son of God, has been forever with the Father—One Who is called the very Word of God?

Think on these things and we'll talk more of this tomorrow.

DAY THREE

The crucifixion of Jesus Christ left the disciples despondent. They could not fathom the death of the One they had believed in! Jesus had told them that although the hour had come for the Son of Man to die, He would be raised from the dead on the third day. But somehow they had missed this truth—or couldn't comprehend it. They missed the sign of Jonah, and grief overwhelmed them.

On the road to Emmaus, Jesus challenged two of His disciples about their faith.

1. Look up Luke 24:13-27, and note what Jesus said to them. Also, note what you learn about the Word of God from this passage.

2. Where did the Bible come from? How was it written? Read 2 Peter 1:20-21 carefully. You might want to write these verses out and explain what they are saying and how they answer those questions.

The Bible is the Word of God. Can you now understand why God wrote what He did through Moses?

> And He humbled you and let you be hungry, and fed you with manna which you did not know, nor did your fathers know, that He might make you understand that man does not live by bread alone, but man lives by everything that proceeds out of the mouth of the LORD (Deuteronomy 8:3).

Consider Deuteronomy 8:3 in light of Habakkuk 2:4. It's obvious that if a man is to live by faith, he must believe everything that comes out of God's mouth and live accordingly.

Therefore, if you, dear child of God, are going to live by faith, you must feed on God's Word.

I believe the reason so many are failing today is that they have not disciplined themselves to read God's Word consistently, day in and day out, and to apply it to every situation in life.

Understanding Habakkuk 2:4 is literally a matter of life and death: eternal life or eternal damnation.

Paul quoted Habakkuk 2:4 in his letter to the Roman believers, and God used that statement to bring Martin Luther, a religious but lost monk, to salvation. His realization of the meaning of Romans 1:17 was then used to set multitudes free from the horrible bondage of a salvation-by-works religion into the glorious freedom of a salvation-by-faith relationship with God Himself.

Habakkuk 2:4 was quoted three times in the New Testament: Romans 1:17, Galatians 3:11, and Hebrews 10:38. It is from these verses that we understand the magnificent sweep of the righteousness that we can have. To be righteous is to be right with God. To live righteously is to live according to what God says is right.

Habakkuk 2:4 was used by New Testament authors in two ways. First, it was used in Romans 1:17 and Galatians 3:11 in relationship to salvation from the penalty of sin to show that salvation comes by faith and not by works. Second, it was used in relationship to the believer's day-by-day salvation from sin's power as he walks by faith, believing and obeying God above all else.

This second aspect of the just living by faith is also seen in Romans 1:17: "For in it [the Gospel] the righteousness of God is revealed from faith to faith; as it is written, 'BUT THE RIGHTEOUS man SHALL LIVE BY FAITH.'" Salvation from sin—whether from the penalty of sin, which is eternal punishment, or from the power of sin's reign in our lives—is always and only by faith. There is no other way a man, woman, or child can be pleasing to God.

Galatians 3:11 says the same thing: "Now that no one is justified by the Law before God is evident." The law can only expose sin. It can never make us righteous!

Righteousness comes only from God. It can *never* be attained by the flesh or by our self-righteous efforts. "He saved us, not on the basis of deeds which we have done in righteousness, but according to His mercy, by the washing of regeneration and renewing by the Holy Spirit" (Titus 3:5). ——

Think about it, dear Christian. What makes you acceptable to God? On what basis do you try to make yourself acceptable to God?

As you walk by faith, you live a righteous life, for righteousness is always by faith.___

As a monk, Martin Luther wished to obtain an indulgence promised by the pope to all who should ascend Pilate's Staircase on their knees. The steps, he was told, had been miraculously transported from Jerusalem to Rome.

Luther kissed each step, begging God's mercy and forgiveness for the sins of his flesh, which tormented him. Suddenly, in the midst of performing this meritorious act, he thought he heard a voice of thunder cry from the bottom of his heart, *"The just shall live by faith."* As these words resounded unceasingly and powerfully within him, Luther rose in amazement from the steps up which he had been dragging his body.

The truth had set him free! Later he wrote, "Although I was a holy and blameless monk, my conscience was nevertheless full of trouble and anguish. I could not endure those words—'the righteousness of God.' I had no love for that holy and just God who punishes sinners. I was filled with secret anger against Him: I hated Him because, not content with frightening by the law and the miseries of life . . . He still further increased our tortures by the gospel . . . But when . . . I learned how the justification of the sinner proceeds from the free mercy of our Lord through faith . . . then I felt born again like a new man; I entered . . . into the very paradise of God. Henceforward, also, I saw the beloved and Holy Scriptures with other eyes . . . .As previously I had detested . . . these words, 'the righteousness of God,' I began from that hour to value and to love them . . . ." [3]

What do *you* think of the righteousness of God? Does it seem an impossible attainment, a goal never to be reached? Do you shudder at your own inability to be holy? Do you understand the righteousness which can be yours *only* if you believe in the Lord Jesus Christ?

To be righteous means to be in right standing with God because your sins have been taken care of! When Christ hung on the cross, it was for your sins. There God "made Him who knew no sin to be sin on our behalf, that we might become the righteousness of God in Him" (2 Corinthians 5:21).

At the moment of faith, the moment of trusting in Christ's substitutionary death for your sins, you are declared righteous. You, like Martin Luther and every other true child of God, begin to live. The just shall live by faith.

But that is just the beginning! You are saved by faith from sin's ultimate penalty, which is eternal death in the lake of fire.

Once that birth takes place, you are to *walk* by faith.

This second aspect of the righteous living by faith is emphasized in Habakkuk 2:4 and in Hebrews 10:38. Both Habakkuk and the recipients of the book of Hebrews were living in difficult times, times of testing. In these times, as always, there was only one way to live, and that was by faith. To live any other way, under any other religious system, philosophy, reasoning, or thinking, would be pride. "Behold, as for the proud one, his soul is not right within him; but the righteous will live by his faith" (Habakkuk 2:4).

No matter what the trial, no matter what the circumstances, you and I are to live by every word that proceeds out of the mouth of God—without compromise. We are to trust and obey; there is no other way.

Are you truly His child? How are you living?

DAY FIVE

We are so used to living in an instant world that it is difficult to wait for anything.

When a significant event takes place somewhere in the world, a flick of the channel selector will soon give us an instant rundown on the situation. If we want something to gratify our appetite, there are plenty of fast-food places, or there is the frozen food section in the grocery store and a microwave to heat or cook it in a hurry. Or we can just add water, shake, or stir.

If we want to buy something and don't have the cash, there are all sorts of ways to buy it on credit, and sometimes the payments won't even begin for several months. Yet, we can have our product immediately.

We're a society that has so promoted and provided instant gratification to the flesh, that to deny ourselves *anything* seems almost cruel. We are no longer an immoral society; we're amoral. Anything goes as long as it makes man happy. There is no fear of God before our eyes.

Man is the center of his own world. What exists, exists for his pleasure. When he wants something, he goes after it. He'll get it for himself. He will do it for himself. Self will be satisfied.

In a world like this, a man or woman who lives by faith is a rarity. Living by faith requires patience, for the one who lives by faith becomes dependent upon God. You no longer call the shots. You no longer operate on your timetable. You don't just rush out to get, to do, to have, to satisfy. You pray. You ask. You seek His will, His counsel. *Then* you wait for God's leadership—His insight, His wisdom, His provision, His answer.

Faith recognizes that God is in control, not man.

Faith does it God's way, in God's timing—according to His good pleasure.

Faith does not take life into its own hands, but, in respect and trust, places it in God's.

This is the contrast between "the proud one [whose] soul is not right within him" and the righteous one who "lives by faith." Faith waits and trusts, taking God at His Word. Pride moves according to its own desires, its own will. Pride does what it wants to do, when it wants to do it, and the way it wants to do it!

How are you living, my friend—in faith or in pride? "The righteous will live by his faith" (Habakkuk 2:4).

When life is difficult to understand, when doubt pounds on the door of your mind calling you a fool for not letting him in, when believing God seems insane, when human reasoning lays before you the rational choices of the majority of thinking men and women, what will you do?

Will you follow the logical choices of man, or will you seek your God in prayer, waiting to see what He will say? And when His answer comes, will you cling to His Word in faith?

When things become difficult, even unbearable, will you change your mood with the tide of circumstances, or will you rejoice in the God of your salvation? In the trial of your faith, will you turn to the arm of flesh, or will you allow God to be your strength? Will you stumble in the darkness of your own reasoning and in the logic of the blind leading the blind, or will you let God help you walk above the difficulties of life?

Listen to Jeremiah 17:5-8:

Thus says the LORD,
"Cursed is the man who trusts in mankind
And makes flesh his strength,
And whose heart turns away from the LORD.
For he will be like a bush in the desert
And will not see when prosperity comes,
But will live in stony wastes in the wilderness,
A land of salt without inhabitant.

Blessed is the man who trusts in the LORD
And whose trust is the LORD.
For he will be like a tree planted by the water,
That extends its roots by a stream
And will not fear when the heat comes;
But its leaves will be green,
And it will not be anxious in a year of drought
Nor cease to yield fruit."

List below what you learned about the cursed and the blessed. Note who is cursed and who is blessed, why, and what will happen to each.

The Cursed	The Blessed

Every difficulty is a test—a test to see whether you will believe God. A trial to drive you into His arms and His promises, where you find Him all-sufficient. That is what the book of Habakkuk is about. In Habakkuk we see the difficulty of wondering where God is when bad things happen, and then the delight of discovering He is there, ruling over all.

Like Habakkuk, all we have to do is lay down our pride.

And choose to live by faith.

DAY SIX

Did you ever expect something from God and receive an answer that didn't happen *the way* you thought it should or *when* you thought it should?

Many Christians say that all we have to do is claim things in faith, believe they are ours, make a positive confession, and they will happen. And if things don't come out the way you have claimed them or confessed them, it's because you don't have enough faith or because someone else has hindered the work of God through a negative confession.

I don't believe such thinking is biblically based. It does not concur with the whole counsel of the Word of God.

Habakkuk could have made a positive confession every minute on the minute. It still wouldn't have changed his circumstances. He could have praised God in faith and claimed victory over the forces of Satan as they sought to bring the Babylonians against Judah, but it would not have altered what was about to take place. Yet some Christians today would say that Habakkuk dropped the ball. They would say things could have been different if Habakkuk had only had enough faith, claimed the right promises, prayed the right prayer, and said the right things.

God will not be manipulated. He does not conform to us or to our estimation of life. Rather, we are to bow the knee in faith and know the sovereign "LORD is in His holy temple. Let all the earth be silent before Him" (Habakkuk 2:20).

When my father had to go into the hospital for surgery on an aortic aneurysm, I asked God for a scripture concerning him. I felt God gave me Psalm 20 and, with it, the assurance that my sixty-eight-year-old father would not die. But almost a month later, after five major operations within twelve days, Daddy died.

I wasn't there. I left him in the intensive care unit with my mother at his side and returned to my family in Chattanooga, believing that he would live.

I felt that I had the Word of God regarding my father. But I was wrong. Daddy died. Had my faith failed? Had God failed? What went wrong?

Nothing went wrong—I simply misunderstood God's plans.

Is something not happening in your life that you think should be happening? Or has something happened that you think God shouldn't have allowed? Are there cries or pleas God doesn't seem to respond to? Write them out below. Put them down where you can see them. Verbalize them before God.

In the light of what you are learning in Habakkuk, are you going to allow this to throw you into a chasm of distress or despair?

Read aloud Isaiah 40:27 and put your name in place of Israel's and Jacob's. Then listen to God's response in 40:28-31. Read it aloud.

Why do you say, O Jacob, and assert, O Israel,
My way is hidden from the LORD,
And the justice due me escapes the
        notice of my God? (Isaiah 40:27).

Do you not know? Have you not heard?
The Everlasting God, the LORD, the Creator
        of the ends of the earth
Does not become weary or tired.
His understanding is inscrutable.
He gives strength to the weary,
And to him who lacks might He increases power.
Though youths grow weary and tired,
And vigorous young men stumble badly,
Yet those who wait for the LORD
Will gain new strength;
They will mount up with wings like eagles,
They will run and not get tired,
They will walk and not become weary
                        (Isaiah 40:28-31).

I will wait for You
like silence waits for sound,
darkness for light . . .
I will wait for You . . . .[4]

DAY SEVEN

When you cry for help and God does not seem to be moving to deliver you out of your trials or your afflictions, what should you do?

You need to do what God told Habakkuk to do: You need to live by faith (Habakkuk 2:4).

Remember that the book of Habakkuk is the record of a questioning soul's conversation with God. It's a conversation that began with a cry of distress and confusion and ended with a prayer of rejoicing. Habakkuk rejoiced—*even though he knew his circumstances would not change.*

The answers God gave Habakkuk were not easy: Deliverance from the enemy was not going to come; a day of distress would not be averted.

That is why Habakkuk said, "I heard and my inward parts trembled, at the sound my lips quivered. Decay enters my bones, and in my place I tremble. Because I must wait quietly for the day of distress, for the people to arise who will invade us" (Habakkuk 3:16).

How then could Habakkuk praise God? Doesn't faith always deliver us out of our trials?

Some would say yes.

I would say not always.

But God *does* promise that you can live as more than a conqueror! Watch, Beloved, for in the book of Habakkuk you will learn lessons of victory that will deliver you *through* trials. When God, for your good and His glory, does not deliver you *out* of a trial, He will teach you how you can walk with hinds' feet on high places.

This is what I've seen time and time again—and sometimes in the lives of people who have lived an almost fairy tale existence—until great trouble swept in like a tidal wave.

149

My friend Janice grew up in an ideal home. She couldn't have asked for more godly, loving parents. When she took her marriage vows, people thought there couldn't have been a more ideal match. The bridegroom loved the Lord and felt called into the ministry. Their children were a delight, their ministry a seeming success.

Then he just walked away.

The "perfect marriage" came to a halt. Janice was shattered—as were her parents. Yet in the midst of it all, Janice clung to her God, to His promises. She determined to walk with hinds' feet on His high places over the valleys of despair. And from that determination a song of faith the Lord had given to Janice in earlier years took on new depth and meaning. Take a few moments and sing the words to the tune of "My Favorite Things" from *The Sound of Music*, and reflect on the song's message.

> Joy through my teardrops, and gains through
> my losses
> Beauty for ashes, and crowns for my crosses;
> He binds my wounds, and He dries all my
> tears
> Calms every storm and He conquers my fears.
>
> He gives me hinds' feet to walk on high places.
> He floods my soul with His heavenly graces;
> When I am weak then His strength makes me
> strong
> I know I can trust Him, He's never been wrong.
>
> Trials may come and temptations assail me
> Though I may falter, He never will fail me;
> So Satan I bind you in His holy name
> For at the cross Jesus' blood overcame!
>
> When the doubt comes, when I'm lonely
> When my heart is sad;

I'll lift up mine eyes to my Saviour above
And Jesus will make me glad.

When in my heart there is sadness and sorrow
Jesus has promised a brighter tomorrow;
Victory is mine, Yes, it's already won
I've only to claim it by faith in God's Son.

All of my cares I will cast down before Him
Even in trials my heart will adore Him;
He bears my burdens, He comforts my soul
Oh why should I worry when He's in control?

Lord in the time of deep grief and emotion
I will yet serve You with constant devotion;
You have not failed me one step of the way
That is the reason I'll trust You and say:

I will praise You! I will praise You!
Jesus Christ my King;
For You fill my heart with a song in the night
Yes, You make my heart to sing!

Now take a few moments to meditate on Isaiah
50:8-10.

He who vindicates Me is near;
Who will contend with Me?
Let us stand up to each other;
Who has a case against Me?
Let him draw near to Me.
Behold, the Lord GOD helps Me;
Who is he who condemns Me?
Behold, they will all wear out like a garment;
The moth will eat them.
Who is among you that fears the LORD,
That obeys the voice of His servant,
That walks in darkness and has no light?
Let him trust in the name of the LORD
and rely on his God.

Now, justified one, live by faith.

Notes

1. W. E. Vine, *Vine's Expository Dictionary of Old and New Testament Words* (Old Tappan, New Jersey: Fleming H. Revell Company, 1981), II, 71.

2. Vine, I, p. 116.

3. J. H. Merle D'Aubigne, *The Life and Times of Martin Luther* (Chicago: Moody Press, 1978), 54-56.

4. Melissa Aguayo, *What I Would Be is Faithful—What I Would Do Is Love You. A Collection of Thoughts*, used by permission.

Chapter 8

HE'S THERE,
WOE TO THE PROUD,
THE GREEDY

DAY ONE

No cruelty, no crime, no injustice escapes the attention of God. He is there when bad things happen. And although God may use evil men or ungodly nations to judge His people or to carry out His eternal purposes, they will be held accountable for what they have done.

The wicked will be punished. This is clearly stated in Habakkuk: "I am raising up the Chaldeans, that fierce and impetuous people who march throughout the earth to seize dwelling places which are not theirs . . . . Then they will sweep through like the wind and pass on. *But they will be held guilty, they whose strength is their god"* (Habakkuk 1:6,11; emphasis added). The book of Jeremiah states, "Indeed Babylon is to fall for the slain of Israel" (Jeremiah 51:49).

This was part of the vision Habakkuk was to record and others were to proclaim. The Lord would justly deal woes to those who treated men like fish, worshiped the nets that caught the fish, and swallowed up those more righteous than they (Habakkuk 1:13-17). Judgment will come when God goes forth for the salvation of His anointed.

We'll see this in the third chapter of Habakkuk. Before that, however, we need to look at the taunt-song (Habakkuk 2:6) against the Babylonians, a song for those who are proud and behave as the Babylonians behaved. In it you'll gain valuable insight into a side of God often neglected: His wrath and just judgment.

Turn to your observation sheets on Habakkuk in the back of this book and carefully read through Habakkuk 2 again. If you have not marked every use of the word *woe*, do so this time.

Now, the taunt-song has five stanzas of three verses each. This type of song is called a *masal*, which is Hebrew poetry employing parallelism. As you read, note the nature of each woe, to whom it will come, and why it is pronounced. Observe all you can and record your insights in the margin next to each woe.

Stop and do this before you read any further.

Those who do not live by faith are considered proud; their soul is not right within them. That's what the Lord God says. Listen again to Habakkuk 2:4 with the ears of faith: "Behold, as for the proud one, his soul is not right within him; but the righteous will live by his faith."

People who are proud refuse to submit to the Word of God. They will not humble themselves under the mighty hand of God. They walk according to their own desires. They are governed by their own reason. *They* decide what is good and what is evil.

The proud run their own lives and will only submit to God when it's convenient for them.. Otherwise, when you confront them with something in the Word they don't want to believe and obey, they say, "Well, that's your interpretation." Or, "It can be interpreted different ways."

The proud don't listen; they attack.

The proud man is haughty. "'Proud,' 'Haughty,' 'Scoffer,' are his names, who acts with insolent pride" (Proverbs 21:24).

The proud one is ruled by his appetite.

These were the Babylonians—a picture of the extreme to which men can go without God. Woe to them, and woe to those who live like them.

God sets before Habakkuk the way of life and death—and the consequences. For those who walk by faith, there's life. For those who are proud, there are woes and death. There's much to learn from these woes. Knowing what Habakkuk says regarding the fate of the wicked will help you understand where God is when bad things happen. You'll see that He's not divorced from your pain.

God is not like others who walk away or don't want to know what's going on. God doesn't stand on the sidelines and refuse to get involved because it is none of His business. Everything that concerns you is His business! He's not a distant creator who brought you into being and then abandoned you, saying, "Good luck growing up, kid. Hope you do all right." He is not only your Creator, He's also your Sustainer.

Nor does He beat up on His kids. He disciplines them, but it is always for their good.

So when you wonder where God is when bad things happen, remember:

1. God is in control. He rules over all. He's in charge of history . . . yours as well as the nations!

2. All history centers on two groups of people: Israel and the Church. If you are in Christ because He is in you, then you are a vital part of the Church, a member of Jesus' body.

3. There is a purpose in what God is doing, whether we see it or not. You have God's promise on that. What happens may not be good, but because He is God, He'll cause it to work together for your good.

4. Your times are in His hands. He's in charge of the timetable, so wait patiently.

5. Fear and doubt are conquered by a faith that rejoices. And faith can rejoice because the promises of God are as certain as God Himself.

And where do the woes fit in? They come under the third principle: **There is a purpose in what God is doing. He is acting according to His character.**

Although Habakkuk could not understand why God allowed the Babylonians to be His instrument of judgment upon His people Israel, God had a purpose in it all. He would use the Babylonians to judge; yet in His righteousness, God would also judge the Babylonians.

Although you, my friend, cannot understand why God did not intervene on your behalf in the midst of your trauma, you must believe God had a purpose. And if evil was done to you, it will be judged. Evil must come, but woe to those by whom it comes.

"For the LORD is a God of recompense, He will fully repay" (Jeremiah 51:56b). And as the Lord says,

"Will not all of these [the peoples and nations captured by the Babylonians] take up a taunt-song against him?" (Habakkuk 2:6). The taunt-song is a reminder that there will be a day when those who suffered at the hands of the Babylonians will see retribution meted out upon their oppressors.

So as you look at these woes, remember that although they are pronounced against the Babylonians, they pertain to all who behave likewise. God is immutable; He never changes. He is consistent not only in blessing the righteous but also in judging sinners.

DAY TWO

Greed is subtle.

It begins with the lust of the eyes as it contemplates what it would be like to possess—more things, more power, more of anything—until you must take from others to satisfy your own appetite. Confronting this, God pronounced His first of the woes on the wicked.

> Will not all of these take up a taunt-song
>   against him, even mockery and insinuations
>   against him,
> And say, "Woe to him who increases what is
>   not his—
> For how long—
> And makes himself rich with loans?"
> Will not your creditors rise up suddenly,
> And those who collect from you awaken?
> Indeed, you will become plunder for them.
> Because you have looted many nations,
> All the remainder of the peoples will loot
>   you—
> Because of human bloodshed and violence
>   done to the land,
> To the town and all its inhabitants"
> (Habakkuk 2:6-8).

Before we go any further, examine what you have read and record your insights so you don't miss what God is saying.

1. What was the Babylonians' motive in conquering other nations?

2. What went along with the looting of others?

3. Who would be considered their creditors or those who collect from them? To answer this, remember who the Babylonians grew rich from. Were the Babylonians taking what was theirs or taking from others?

4. Would the Babylonians get away with it? What happened to them?

5. Are there any principles in these verses that can be applied to those seeking to be rich? What get-rich tactics do you see that are wrong?

The King James Version translates the Greek word for *greed* as *covetousness*. In essence they are one and the same. Covetousness is expressly forbidden in the

Ten Commandments. "You shall not covet your neighbor's house; you shall not covet your neighbor's wife or his male servant or his female servant or his ox or his donkey or anything that belongs to your neighbor" (Exodus 20:17).

The Babylonians coveted what the other nations had so they went after it—and brutally wrenched it from the homes of the people they conquered. They took things they had not labored or saved for. They stole other men's wives and children for their own pleasure and service. They hauled away treasures that belonged to families, treasures that held precious memories. They wasted homes, forests, property—but mostly lives, as they left a trail of blood—all because of greed. They were totally occupied with self—their pleasures, their happiness, their comfort, their conveniences. What they had didn't satisfy them. It wasn't enough.

Have you, my friend, been a victim of another's greed? Have you lost a husband or a wife because someone else coveted him or her? Remember how God rebuked King David through Nathan the prophet after David stole Uriah's wife Bathsheba, and then as if that weren't enough, took Uriah's life? Take a few minutes and read the story Nathan used to point out David's sin. You'll find it in 2 Samuel 12:1-11.

1. How did the story illustrate what David had done?

2. How does this illustrate covetousness or greed?

3. In this story, who was the debtor? That is, who owed what, and why?

4. What was David's solution?

When the Babylonians took what was not theirs, they became the debtors, and the people they stole from were the creditors. The Babylonians owed a debt to those they looted. Eventually the debt would be paid, because God is a just judge.

DAY THREE

How do you, my friend, view money and the accumulation of earthly possessions? Have you ever stopped to think about it? Since we are looking at the woes of those who seek to make themselves rich at the expense of others, I think we need to consider the Christian's attitude toward wealth and treasures.

Is it a sin to be rich—to possess material things? Let's discover what the Word of God has to say.

In 1 John 2:15-17 we read:

Do not love the world, nor the things in the world. If anyone loves the world, the love of the Father is not in him. For all that is in the world, the lust of the flesh and the lust of the eyes and the boastful pride of life, is not from the Father, but is from the world. And the world is passing away, and also its lusts; but the one who does the will of God abides forever.

What is expressly forbidden in these verses? Be specific in your answer.

Next, look at 1 Timothy 6:7-12,17-19. As you read, mark every reference to "rich" or "riches."

For we have brought nothing into the world, so we cannot take anything out of it either. And if we have food and covering, with these we shall be content. But those who want to get rich fall into temptation and a snare and many foolish and harmful desires which plunge men into ruin and destruction. For the love of money is a root of all sorts of evil, and some by longing for it have wandered away from the faith, and pierced themselves with many a pang. But flee from these things, you man of God; and pursue righteousness, godliness, faith, love, perseverance and gentleness.

Fight the good fight of faith; take hold of the eternal life to which you were called, and you made the good confession in the presence of many witnesses. . . . Instruct those who are rich in this present world not to be conceited or to fix their hope on the uncertainty of riches, but on God, who richly supplies us with all things to enjoy. Instruct them to do good, to be rich in good works, to be generous and ready to share, storing up for themselves the treasure of a good foundation for the future, so that they may take hold of that which is life indeed.

When Paul tells Timothy to "flee from these things," he is referring to more than the love of money. Since greed is our subject, however, this is where we want to keep our focus.

Read through the following questions before you attempt to answer them, as they may overlap one another in their answers.

1. What are we to be content with?

2. Is it wrong to be rich—to have money? Explain your answer.

3. What *is* wrong? Why?

4. What are God's instructions through Paul to those who are rich? What will be the end result of walking in obedience to the Lord?

5. What are you pursuing? Or, to put it another way, what are your goals in life?

Have you ever thought of greed as a form of idolatry?

That's what God calls greed in the New Testament. Listen: "Therefore consider the members of your earthly body as dead to immorality, impurity, passion, evil desire, and greed, which amounts to [literally, *is*] idolatry. For it is on account of these things that the wrath of God will come, and in them you also once walked, when you were living in them" (Colossians 3:5-7).

Interesting, isn't it? When we think of idolatry, we usually think of people worshiping images fashioned by their own hands. Or we think of sticks, stones, or fetishes of one sort or another. But greed! If it were not stated in the Word of God, would anyone think of it as idolatry? Probably not, unless we recognize an idol as anything that takes God's rightful place in our allegiance, devotion, time, or energies.

Let me ask you several questions so we can reason together. If a Christian doesn't have time to study God's Word and pray but has time for television, would you call that idolatry? Or if a child of God finds time to exercise, work out, do aerobics, play on a church softball or basketball team, but doesn't have time to spend with God in His Word and in prayer, would you call that idolatry? Or if a Christian has time to work longer hours or take on a second job to have more money for more things but doesn't have time for the Lord, would you call that idolatry?

You may be saying, "But people need to earn extra money just in case something happens." Or, "All my life I've wanted such and such and I'm going after it—I deserve it."

We've already looked at what the Word of God says about riches. Today let's look at what God says about laying up treasures and trusting Him.

Printed out below is Matthew 6:19-34. Read it carefully, and mark the following words each in a distinctive way or color so you can spot them at a glance:

1. treasures in heaven
2. treasures upon earth
3. eye
4. anxious
5. God or Father and the appropriate pronouns
6. mammon (another word for riches)

After you read the passage, answer the questions which follow.

MATTHEW 6:19-34

Do not lay up for yourselves treasures upon earth, where moth and rust destroy, and where thieves break in and steal. But lay up for yourselves treasures in heaven, where neither moth nor rust destroys, and where thieves do not break in or steal; for where your treasure is, there will your heart be also. The lamp of the body is the eye; if therefore your eye is clear, your whole body will be full of light. But if your eye is bad, your whole body will be full of darkness. If therefore the light that is in you is darkness, how great is the darkness! No one can serve two masters; for either he will hate the one and love the other, or he will hold to one and despise the other. You cannot serve God and mammon. For this reason I say to you, do not be anxious for your life, as to what you shall eat, or what you shall drink; nor for your body, as to what you shall put on. Is not life more than food, and the body than clothing? Look at the birds of the air, that they do not sow, neither do they reap, nor gather into barns, and yet your heavenly Father feeds them. Are you not worth much more than they? And which of you by being anxious can add a single cubit to his life's span? And why are you anxious about clothing? Observe how the lilies of the field grow; they do not toil nor do they spin, yet I say to you that even Solomon in all his glory did not clothe himself like one of these. But if God so arrays the grass of the field, which is alive today and tomorrow is thrown into the furnace, will He not much more do so for you, O men of little faith? Do not be anxious then, saying, "What shall we eat?" or "What shall we drink?" or "With what shall we clothe ourselves?" For all these things the Gentiles eagerly seek; for your heavenly Father knows that you need all these things. But seek first His kingdom and His righteousness; and all these things shall be added to you. Therefore do not be anxious for tomorrow; for tomorrow will care for itself. Each day has enough trouble of its own.

1. What do you learn about treasures from this portion of Matthew?

2. Why did Jesus talk about the eye in this passage? What point was He making? Does it fit in with anything else you have studied these past days?

3. What do you learn about serving God and riches? Can you see any relationship between this and what you learned yesterday? Explain.

4. List the things mentioned in this passage that a person might be anxious about. Next to each, write out why you think a person would be anxious about that particular thing.

5. Are we to be anxious about these things? Why?

6. To whom do you think this passage is addressed and why?

7. List our Lord's admonitions to you in this passage. Next to each write out your reason for obeying or disobeying them.

Well, friend, that's it for another day. How has our Lord spoken to you in these past three days as you studied the first of His five woes? Have you been convicted about anything? It's good to write it down so you don't forget it.

Day Five

Has the company you've worked for all these years suddenly fired you when you were on the brink of retiring? Have they pocketed your retirement so they can save their own neck financially?

Has your home ever been robbed? Has anything ever been stolen from you? Have you been swindled before? Woe upon that person, for he did exactly what the Babylonians did to Judah.

Has anyone ever told a lie against you in order to keep you from something or someone he wanted?

Has anyone ever put you down so he could look better? Do you think these things escape the notice of a holy God, Who neither slumbers nor sleeps, but Who, from His throne on high, beholds all the affairs of men?

The second woe is against those who seek their own security at another's expense:

> Woe to him who gets evil gain for his house
> To put his nest on high
> To be delivered from the hand of calamity!
> You have devised a shameful thing for your
> house
> By cutting off many peoples;
> So you are sinning against yourself.
> Surely the stone will cry out from the wall,
> And the rafter will answer it from the framework
> (Habakkuk 2:9-11).

The Babylonians were building their kingdom at the expense of other people. They thought that by destroying others and strengthening their own kingdom, they would secure themselves against the aggression of other nations. They forgot it is God who "removes kings and establishes kings" (Daniel 2:21).

This second woe condemns self-exaltation, the putting of one's self above another for the sake of your own good, your own benefit, your own security.

How contrary to the example we have in our Lord Jesus Christ! The mind of Christ is the opposite of pride or self-exaltation. It is laying aside selfishness and regarding others as more important than ourselves. It is taking on the role of servant rather than master. It is laying down your life for another.

While woe comes upon those who exalt themselves at the expense of others, God promises blessing for those who don't do that. Read Philippians 2:3-11, which follows this paragraph. Read it prayerfully. Ask God to show you if you need cleansing through this portion of His Word.

Do nothing from selfishness or empty conceit, but with humility of mind let each of you regard one another as more important than himself; do not merely look out for your own personal interests, but also for the interests of others. Have this attitude in yourselves which was also in Christ Jesus, who, although He existed in the form of God, did not regard equality with God a thing to be grasped, but emptied Himself, taking the form of a bond-servant, and being made in the likeness of men. And being found in appearance as a man, He humbled Himself by becoming obedient to the point of death, even death on a cross. Therefore also God highly exalted Him, and bestowed on Him the name which is above every name, that at the name of Jesus EVERY KNEE SHOULD BOW, of those who are in heaven, and on earth, and under the earth, and that every tongue should confess that Jesus Christ is Lord, to the glory of God the Father.

Read through this passage again; then read the next three questions before you answer them.

What are God's specific instructions to the believer?

Now, read the passage once more. What was Jesus' attitude? How was it manifested?

Just before our Lord was betrayed, He gathered His disciples in the upper room. Remember that in those days slaves washed the feet of all who entered a house. But since the upper room had been rented by the disciples, there was no slave to wash their feet. Then Jesus "rose from supper . . . taking a towel, He girded Himself . . . poured water . . . and began to wash the disciples' feet" (John 13:4-5). When He finished, He said, "I gave you an example that you also should do as I did to you" (v. 15). This is the example of the One Whom they called Teacher and Lord. And He would give them yet an even greater example when He laid down His life for them. Love wears a towel.

Are there any aspects of your attitude or your relationships with others in which you've been more like the Babylonians than like Jesus? Allow the Lord to search your heart. He'll do it in love. He simply wants a clean temple.

"If we judged ourselves rightly, we should not be judged. But when we are judged, we are disciplined by the Lord in order that we may not be condemned along with the world" (1 Corinthians 11:31-32).

As we conclude our study of the second woe, we need to remember: When greedy men build their own houses through evil gain and at the expense of others, people will cry out *Where is God?* Our answer to them is that the very stones of the house will cry out and the rafters will answer. Habakkuk 2:11 tells us that whatever was obtained through evil will testify against the evildoer. There is *nothing* hidden which will not be brought to light.

When I look at the five woes of Habakkuk, I see a progressive worsening in evil, moving from one action bringing judgment to the next. Take a few moments and read through Habakkuk 2:6-20 again and write out how one sin, left unchecked, leads to the other.

The proud, evil lifestyle of the wicked begins with greed, which in turn leads to a self-exaltation which cuts off others. Then, because self is exalted above others, what else would you expect? Violence and bloodshed. Not only do you steal what others have so you can have more—you abuse anyone who gets in the way of self!

Drunk on self and power, you then seduce your neighbors for your own sensual satisfaction. And why not?! The idols you worship don't condemn you! And God, if there is a God, doesn't notice or get involved in the affairs of mere men!

It is almost as if when a person (or a nation) gets caught up in a state of covetousness or greed, he is trapped in a downward spiral of evil. And the root of it all is the lust of unrestrained flesh—unleashed passion which "enlarges his appetite like Sheol, and . . . is like death, never satisfied" (Habakkuk 2:5).

Greed is enslaving. The more you have, the more you want—until eventually avarice consumes you. Then whatever it costs, whatever it takes to satisfy your hunger, you'll do it. Greed can cause a man to put his desires above the welfare of another, to go after what he wants without concern for others, and to take what is not his—even if it requires shedding blood.

But greed doesn't stop there . . . it is *consuming*. Once man has all the stuff he desires, he entices his neighbor so that he might satisfy his sensual desires. Why? Because his god is his appetite and his glory is his shame. There is no fear of God before his eyes; therefore, "his soul is not right within him" (Habakkuk 2:4). His corruption spills over onto others.

Listen and note how this third woe follows upon the other two: "Woe to him who builds a city with bloodshed and founds a town with violence! Is it not indeed from the LORD of hosts that peoples toil for fire, and nations grow weary for nothing?" (Habakkuk 2:12-13).

Think about it. And tomorrow, we'll go into greater depth on this third woe.

Day Seven

Those who watch network television for more than two hours on any given night rarely escape being exposed to violence and bloodshed. The statistics concerning the amount of violence and crime seen by the average child before he reaches puberty are constantly changing from one year to the next—and become increasingly alarming. Is it any wonder that our children are desensitized to violence and evil at a very early age? And when the television is turned off and they go to their toy boxes or turn on their video games, does the exposure to violence cease? Sadly, no.

You cannot take in all that violence, profanity, and immorality without it searing your conscience to one degree or another and influencing your perspective of life. What the eyes and ears take in, the mind and heart feed upon. Here again we see that as a man thinks, so he is (Proverbs 23:7).

Consider Matthew 15:18-19 in the light of the subjects we've been discussing. Write out what you learn from these verses.

Why are we plagued with teenage immorality, pregnancies, and abortions? Why are condoms the issue and not abstinence? It is because we have become an amoral society. Man and his pleasures have moved God from His rightful place. We have slain the absolutes of God upon the altar of our lusts. We have abandoned purity.

As a nation where well over one million babies are aborted every year, are we not a land of cities filled with bloodshed? We then use their little aborted bodies for cosmetics to make us more beautiful—bodies conceived on beds of adultery. Isn't this violence and injustice?

Is it not violent to kill an innocent and helpless—but feeling—child, cutting him into pieces then using a vacuum to suck the parts from the womb? Is it not violent to invade his haven with a sharp curettage, whipping it round and round as you'd beat up an egg? Is it not violent to rotate that instrument until it cuts him off from his supply of oxygen, leaving no way of escape as he's chased around his mother's womb until his body is cut into tiny pieces that will convulsively, but quietly, seep out of the sanctuary where he was conceived by the knowledge and will of God?

Is it not violent to inject a saline solution into the security of a mother's womb in order to sear and burn the flesh of an unwanted child, to cause the baby to thrash and writhe in anguish until he's burned to death?

Is it not violent to destroy what God has chosen to weave in a mother's womb, given life by God's own breath (Psalm 139:13-16)?

Where is God? Why does He allow this to continue? Why does our justice system put people who protest such bloodshed and violence in jail, yet turn murderers and rapists loose to murder and rape again? Why do the wicked seem to be victorious in all the wanton bloodshed left on the trail of their own pursuit of happiness?

Habakkuk asked God the same questions. "How long, O LORD, will I call for help, and Thou wilt not hear? I cry out to Thee, 'Violence!' Yet Thou dost not save. Why dost Thou make me see iniquity, and cause me to look on wickedness? Yes, destruction and violence are before me; strife exists and contention arises. Therefore, the law is ignored and justice is never upheld. For the wicked surround the righteous; therefore, justice comes out perverted" (Habakkuk 1:2-4).

Then came the vision . . . and Habakkuk understood.

And someday, *everyone* will understand, for the earth will be filled with the knowledge of the glory of the Lord, as the waters cover the sea. Someday men will see that, all the time, the Lord was in His holy temple. God knew what was going on.

Men and nations may build their domains through violence and bloodshed, but there will be a day of reckoning. God says that they are toiling for fire (Habakkuk 2:13).

What they gain will someday be destroyed. God will devour it in judgment. For "the day of the Lord will come like a thief . . . the elements will be destroyed with intense heat, and the earth and its works will be burned up" (2 Peter 3:10).

And when the earth is destroyed, those who do not know Christ, whether they be kings or ordinary men, slaves or free, will be cast into the lake of fire where the worm will not die, nor will the fire be quenched. There they will remain for all eternity (Matthew 25:41,46; Mark 9:44,46,48; Revelation 20:11-15).

Now as we bring this to a close, there's one final thought I must share with you. Violence and bloodshed are not always the end product of greed. You'll find that frequently violence and bloodshed come from anger.

Anger is never to control us. Although God is fully aware of the injustice and cruelty of men, He says, "BE ANGRY, and yet DO NOT SIN; do not let the sun go down on your anger, and do not give the devil an opportunity" (Ephesians 4:26-27). To allow anger to stay within, to not act in faith and deal with it in God's way, can destroy you and others. As I said, it can even lead to violence and bloodshed. For that reason Jesus tells us, "Everyone who is angry with his brother shall be guilty" (Matthew 5:22) because anger that simmers within is like committing murder in your heart.

Oh, Beloved, what has been done to you by another may be evil and unrighteous. Your anger may be righteous anger. But if your soul is going to be right within you, if you are going to live by faith, then you must forgive, give your anger to God, and believe Him when He says it will work together for your good in order to make you more like Jesus (Romans 8:28-29).

Just remember: anger unresolved will only bring you woe.

How is it with your soul today? Is it right within you and before God, or have you stifled your anger? [1]

Give your anger to Him. The guilty will not go unpunished. A righteous God will come to your defense and vindicate you in His time and His way. Walk by faith. Therefore, "Let all bitterness and wrath and anger and clamor and slander be put away from you, along with all malice. And be kind to one another, tender-hearted, forgiving each other, just as God in Christ also has forgiven you" (Ephesians 4:31-32).

"Therefore, since we receive a kingdom which cannot be shaken, let us show gratitude, by which we may offer to God an acceptable service with reverence and awe; for our God is a consuming fire" (Hebrews 12:28-29).

Note

1. If you are having trouble dealing with your anger, you may want to obtain a copy of my book *Lord, Heal My Hurts.* In it you will find a comprehensive and practical study dealing with anger, bitterness, rejection, and other troublesome thoughts and emotions.

Chapter 9

HE'S THERE,
WOE TO
THE DRUNKARD

DAY ONE

One of the ways our country is being destroyed from within is through sexual perversions. If I didn't know and understand that all sin will be justly judged, dealt with, and paid for, I wouldn't be able to handle the righteous indignation that wells up within my soul. But I know that all those who "look on the nakedness of another" will someday look straight into the eyes of God and give an account to Him for their deeds.

The fourth woe is taken up as a taunt-song against

those who entice others and seduce them for their own benefit. It's not only a woe to the Babylonians, but also to every human being who uses another for his own pleasure—to every drug dealer; to every producer, publisher, and seller of pornography; to every person who encourages another to have a drink; to every person who goads another until he joins him in his evil deeds.

It is a woe to every person who has beaten, verbally abused, or sexually misused another person . . . and who in the process destroys lives, leaving them devastated and barren apart from God's grace. It is a word not only to the drunken Babylonians who excused their behavior in the name of conquest, but to every person who might think that, because he was drunk, he was not responsible for his behavior.

Listen once again, dear friend, to the vision God gave Habakkuk. Read it and hurry to proclaim it before society is totally destroyed.

Woe to you who make your neighbors drink,
Who mix in your venom even to make them drunk
So as to look on their nakedness!
You will be filled with disgrace rather than honor. Now you yourself drink and expose your own nakedness.
The cup in the LORD's right hand will come around to you,
And utter disgrace will come upon your glory.
For the violence done to Lebanon will overwhelm you, and the devastation of its beasts
by which you terrified them,
Because of human bloodshed and violence done to the land,
To the town and all its inhabitants
(Habakkuk 2:15-17).

The drinking described in those verses doesn't indicate they've simply had a drink or two—rather, it's a drunkenness that exposes their nakedness. This happened to Noah. Noah began farming, planted a vineyard, drank of the wine "and became drunk, and uncovered himself inside his tent." And his son "saw the nakedness" (Genesis 9:20-22).

While I believe Habakkuk's fourth woe goes beyond simply describing drunkenness and refers to the exposure of Babylon and her judgment as a nation, it is interesting that God uses her love and abuse of wine to illustrate what He's going to do. This isn't the first time Habakkuk mentioned alcohol in reference to the Babylonians. In 2:5 we read that "wine betrays the haughty man, so that he does not stay at home."

Since Habakkuk talked about drinking and drunkenness, and because it is not only a nationwide but a worldwide problem, let's see how a righteous man is to live by faith in respect to alcohol. If we're going to live by faith, we need to know what God's Word has to say on the subject. It will take us a few days, but it will be worth it.

The Babylonians were known for their drinking. One historian said of them: "The Babylonians give themselves wholly to wine, and the things which follow drunkenness."[1] Daniel 5 gives some interesting insight along this line also. Take a few minutes to read Daniel 5. Then record below what you learn from this chapter about the Babylonians—how they behaved, what they worshiped, and what happened to them.

It was during this feast that Darius the Mede took over the Babylonian kingdom and King Belshazzar was killed. History tells us that the Medes attacked while the Babylonians were having their feast and imbibing their wine.

Usually people who drink do not want to drink alone, unless, of course, they are afraid they'll be found out. To the Babylonians, drinking and drunkenness were acceptable. From Habakkuk 2:15 we see that they even enticed their neighbors to join in. What were their motives? To look on another's nakedness.

Where you find alcohol, you often find immorality and destruction, for when a person drinks excessively, he usually loses his inhibitions. The alcohol controls the person, rather than the person controlling the alcohol.

The violence and destruction which many times go hand in hand with alcohol are seen in Habakkuk 2:17, where God says, "For the violence done to Lebanon will overwhelm you, and the devastation of its beasts by which you terrified them, because of human bloodshed and violence done to the land, to the town and all its inhabitants." When the Babylonians conquered Lebanon, they wantonly destroyed Lebanon's people and animals. They also destroyed Lebanon's beautiful forests, leaving just tree stumps.

Because alcohol is a major problem in many countries, we must know what God says about the subject so we can live accordingly. Then we can proclaim it to others—just as Habakkuk was to inscribe these woes on tablets so they could be read and proclaimed to others.

DAY TWO

"Wine betrays the haughty man, so that he does not stay at home" (Habakkuk 2:5). The Babylonians gave their neighbors drink so that they could make them drunk and look on their nakedness (2:15).

Obviously these are consequences of strong drink, but does this make consuming strong drink wrong? What does the Word of God have to say?

Let's look at some other scriptures. Regardless of how you and I may feel about the subject of alcohol, we must be willing to handle the Word of God with integrity. To handle the Word with integrity is to allow the Bible to say what it says without adding to it or taking away from it.

In Isaiah 5, God pronounced some woes on Israel that relate to drinking. As you look at these, you need to be aware that God was angry with His chosen people because they had forgotten Him and were living lives which were very displeasing to Him. He said:

Woe to those who rise early in the morning
    that they may pursue strong drink;
Who stay up late in the evening
    that wine may inflame them!
And their banquets are accompanied by lyre
    and harp, by tambourine and flute, and by
    wine;
But they do not pay attention to the deeds of
    the LORD,
Nor do they consider the work of His hands
    (5:11-12).

When a person makes drinking a priority in the morning or evening and does not make time for the things of God—or neglects what God wants him to do—woes are going to come. A few verses later in Isaiah we read, "Woe to those who are heroes in drinking wine, and valiant men in mixing strong drink" (5:22).

He's There, Woe to the Drunkard

I remember well my B.C. (before Christ) days and the fraternity parties I attended. Although I had set standards regarding alcohol—that I would never get drunk and that I wouldn't allow my date to get drunk—still a lot of the fraternity brothers whom we ran around with loved to have their beer. We'd get in the lounge of the fraternity house and start a round of songs until we inevitably came to the song which challenged someone's ability to empty their beer stein.

We chanted "So drink chug-a-lug, chug-a-lug, chug-a-lug," over and over as a beer stein bearing the "hero's" name above the fraternity's insignia was tipped bottoms up. With a red face, and his sleeve for a napkin, the "hero" would rub his arm across his face to wipe away the foam which spilled over his jaws, and bask in the acclamation of his peers. He was the man of the moment—after all, he'd downed all that beer without pausing for a breath!

What manner of hero was this? What was his destiny? And what of the young woman sitting there whose turn came next? Isaiah says that many a valiant man has known sorrow from mixing strong drink.

What is your position on alcohol? Why? Write out your answer, for it will benefit you to verbalize your stand. When we don't set standards, we may suddenly find ourselves in compromising situations where expediency takes over rather than sound judgment.

How many graduation parties have turned into tragedies because of the death of revellers who mixed alcohol with driving? Or worse still, caused the death of another or left someone maimed or scarred for life?

One act of folly, one indiscretion, one "I might as well," one "Okay, I'll just try it once," becomes the detour leading to a hellish life for the drinker and for others. Almost without exception, their loved ones and sometimes total strangers are affected by the decision to take a drink.

Not too long ago I sat across the table from a beautiful young woman who needed to talk. Brought up to fear God and having professed Christ, she allowed a friend to fix her up with a blind date. Joining the crowd, she ordered a drink. The next morning she woke up in bed with a stranger. Her virginity was gone, never to be regained. Her date had put knock-out drops in her drink.

She never really knew what exactly happened. She felt worthless. Her entire perspective on life changed because of one drink. The consequences of her action were overriding everything she knew about the Word of God. Instead of remembering and clinging to the promises of forgiveness and embracing the lovingkindnesses of God which are new every morning, instead of trusting in His compassions which never fail, she has locked herself in the despair of that one night.

She is not alone. The streets of cities all over the world are inhabited by countless, nameless faces of all ages—men, women, and even children—who would be different if they had not taken that first drink of alcohol. These are people who are either ignorant of the forgiveness and freedom from slavery offered by our Lord Jesus Christ, or who know about it but won't embrace it in faith.

"Wine is a mocker, strong drink a brawler, and whoever is intoxicated by it is not wise" (Proverbs 20:1).

Wine and strong drink can make you do things you normally would not do. It affects your thinking. "'Come,' they say, 'let us get wine, and let us drink heavily of strong drink; and tomorrow will be like today, only more so'" (Isaiah 56:12).

DAY THREE

I love a good ol' western movie. I got that, I guess, from my daddy, because watching a western with him was one of my favorite pastimes. If you watched long enough, eventually you would find ol' Doc having to remove a bullet without an anesthetic. With no other way to deaden the pain, Doc would give his patient a big slug of whiskey.

Doc was no fool; he knew alcohol was a narcotic. It numbs the senses. It makes you feel good for a while, even though you feel bad. It causes you to forget your pain. And it's relaxing. This is why a lot of people drink. Life becomes a vicious battle to stay on top physically—to keep that high so they can function. So they crave alcohol more and more.

Does God's Word acknowledge these things about alcohol? Note the end results of alcohol's narcotic-like effect:

It is not for kings, O Lemuel,
It is not for kings to drink wine,
Or for rulers to desire strong drink,
Lest they drink and forget what is decreed,
And pervert the rights of all the afflicted.
Give strong drink to him who is perishing,
And wine to him whose life is bitter.
Let him drink and forget his poverty,
And remember his trouble no more
(Proverbs 31:4-7).

Take a good look at these verses, then list below everything that you learn from this passage about the effects of alcohol.

According to these verses, it seems that wine, or strong drink, is only for the dying or for those whose life is bitter. Is this passage, then, teaching that alcohol should be given to those who are dying or are in bitterness of life? I don't believe so, because it would contradict other precepts of Scripture.

For instance, in Philippians 4:11-13, Paul indicates that he learned how to be content even when he was in great need. He saw that he could bear all things through Christ Who strengthened him. Escaping pain or distress through alcohol is a slap in the face of your all-sufficient God.

What are your needs? Whom do you think you can really depend on to ultimately and totally fulfill them? Think about it. Pray about it.

DAY FOUR

Have you ever been around someone who was drunk? Sometimes they are sadly humorous. Other times they're embarrassingly obnoxious—or cruel and abusive.

Proverbs 23:29-35 gives a graphic description of the effects of too much drink.

Who has woe? Who has sorrow?
Who has contentions? Who has complaining?

Who has wounds without cause?
Who has redness of eyes?
Those who linger long over wine,
Those who go to taste mixed wine.
Do not look on the wine when it is red,
When it sparkles in the cup,
When it goes down smoothly;
At the last it bites like a serpent,
And stings like a viper.
Your eyes will see strange things,
And your mind will utter perverse things.
And you will be like one who lies down
   in the middle of the sea,
Or like one who lies down on the top of a
   mast.
"They struck me, but I did not become ill;
They beat me, but I did not know it.
When shall I awake?
I will seek another drink."

List below what you learn from these verses about:

1. the effects of alcohol

2. the addictive effect of alcohol

What do you learn from this passage about when not to drink wine?

Just reading these verses reminds me of the alcoholics I came into contact with during my nursing career. How my heart went out to them! How I wish I had known the Lord Jesus Christ then so that I might have introduced them to the One Who could set them free from their slavery to sin (John 8:34-36)! But at that time, I was a slave myself, though I didn't realize it.

Maybe you know someone who has a problem with alcohol. Why don't you spend some time interceding for him or her? Ask the Holy Spirit to show you how to pray. As a matter of fact, why don't you write down that prayer below.

DAY FIVE

If "wine betrays the haughty man," what should be the Christian's relationship to wine or strong drink?

We know from Ephesians 5:18 that we are not to be "drunk with wine, for that is dissipation." To be dissipated is to be out of control. The Christian is never to be out of the control of the Holy Spirit. You cannot be filled with the Holy Spirit and be under the influence of alcohol. Joy and peace do not come from alcohol, they come from obedience to the indwelling Spirit of God.

Drunkenness, according to Galatians 5:19-21, is a deed of the flesh. Let's look carefully at God's Word: "Now the deeds of the flesh are evident, which are: immorality, impurity, sensuality, idolatry, sorcery, enmities, strife, jealousy, outbursts of anger, disputes, dissensions, factions, envying, drunkenness, carousing, and things like these, of which I forewarn you just as I have forewarned you that those who practice such things shall not inherit the kingdom of God."

The verb "practice" is *prasso* in the Greek, and means "to do as a habit or a practice." So it's clear that habitual drunkenness and Christianity are incompatible.

If drunkenness is your habit of life, you can know that you have *not* been born again. That is what God says, not what I think. Listen: "Or do you not know that the unrighteous shall not inherit the kingdom of God? Do not be deceived; neither fornicators, nor idolaters, nor adulterers, nor effeminate, nor homosexuals, nor thieves, nor the covetous, nor *drunkards*, nor revilers, nor swindlers, shall inherit the kingdom of God" (1 Corinthians 6:9-10; emphasis added).

God is not talking in this passage about people who get caught in such sins, but people whose lifestyle is so characterized by these sins that this is what they *are*.

How careful we have to be in these times when so many have embraced what psychology or medicine says rather than clinging to the Word of God! Remember, God made us. He knows man's frame—He's not ignorant of our psychological make up. He's told us we are soul, spirit and body. Nor is God ignorant of medicine—His name is *Jehovah Rapha,* the God who heals. He heals men whom doctors can't heal. Our human knowledge must never replace or contradict the Word of God.

Beware, then, that you don't rationalize and excuse drunkenness as a disease rather than dealing with it as sin. Even though alcoholism can be seen as addictive or as a weakness because of some chemical imbalance within a person, it does not mean it is a disease.

What God calls sin, we must call sin! When we name sin for what it is, men will be able to see God's cure for it.

Listen to 1 Corinthians 6:11: "And such were some of you; but you were washed, but you were sanctified, but you were justified in the name of the Lord Jesus Christ, and in the Spirit of our God." Jesus sets us free from sin. "If therefore the Son shall make you free, you shall be free indeed" (John 8:36).

First Corinthians 6:11 comes right after verses 9 and 10, so open your Bible and read them all together. Then don't forget where these verses are so you can proclaim them to others.

Galatians 5:16 tells us how to walk victoriously in this freedom, even though our flesh may cry out at times for satisfaction. Write this verse out in the space that follows. By the way, the verb *walk* is in the present tense, which denotes continual or habitual action.

Now, what did you learn about controlling the flesh? Can Christians have victory? How? Write your insights.

DAY SIX

There's much debate among Christians about drinking. Some feel that taking mixed drinks is forbidden, but that drinking wine is all right. "As a matter of fact," they point out, "the Christians in Europe and other countries drink wine like we drink water, coffee, or Coke. It's part of their meal!"

What does the Word teach about the Christian's relationship to wine?

As far as I know, nowhere does the Bible expressly forbid drinking wine.

But does the absence of such a command allow you or me the *liberty* of drinking wine?

The answer is found in Romans 14. This chapter appears below for your convenience. Read it carefully. Note and mark in a distinctive way the references to those weak in the faith and to the others who are not named but who understand their liberty in Christ. When you finish, write down what this chapter says with respect to drinking wine.

ROMANS 14

Now accept the one who is weak in faith, but not for the purpose of passing judgment on his opinions. One man has faith that he may eat all things, but he who is weak eats vegetables only. Let not him who eats regard with contempt him who does not eat, and let not him who does not eat judge him who eats, for God has accepted him. Who are you to judge the servant of another? To his own master he stands or falls; and stand he will, for the Lord is able to make him stand. One man regards one day above another, another regards every day alike. Let each man be fully convinced in his own mind. He who observes the day, observes it for the Lord, and he who eats, does so for the Lord, for he gives thanks to God; and he who eats not, for the Lord he does not eat, and gives thanks to God. For not one of us lives for himself, and not one dies for himself; for if we live, we live for the Lord, or if we die, we die for the Lord; therefore whether we live or die, we are the Lord's. For to this end Christ died and lived again, that He might be Lord both of the dead and of the living. But you, why do you judge your brother? Or you again, why do you regard your brother with contempt? For we shall all stand before the judgment seat of God.

For it is written,

"As I live, says the Lord, every knee shall bow to Me, and every tongue shall give praise to God." So then each one of us shall give account of himself to God.

Therefore let us not judge one another anymore, but rather determine this—not to put an obstacle or a stumbling block in a brother's way. I know and am convinced in the Lord Jesus that nothing is unclean in itself; but to him who thinks anything to be unclean, to him it is unclean. For if because of food your brother is hurt, you are no longer walking according to love. Do not destroy with your food him for whom Christ died. Therefore do not let what is for you a good thing be spoken of as evil; for the kingdom of God is not eating and drinking, but righteousness and peace and joy in the Holy Spirit. For he who in this way serves Christ is acceptable to God and approved by men. So then let us pursue the things which make for peace and the building up of one another. Do not tear down the work of God for the sake of food. All things indeed are clean, but they are evil for the man who eats and gives offense. It is good not to eat meat or to drink wine, or to do anything by which your brother stumbles. The faith which you have, have as your own conviction before God. Happy is he who does not condemn himself in what he approves. But he who doubts is condemned if he eats, because his eating is not from faith; and whatever is not from faith is sin.

Taking God at His word is sometimes easier said than done—especially when you're not sure about what the Bible says on a particular subject. Things are not always black and white. The Christian life is not always spelled out in specific commands which cover all aspects of life. There are precepts—standards and principles of life—which need to be discerned that help us make it through the maze of the gray areas. And even as we seek His way, we need to be careful we do not force our standards on others or judge them by the liberties we exercise as children of God.

This was the situation confronting the church at Rome. The church was composed of Jews and Gentiles, each bringing with them a different heritage. The Gentiles came from a background of little moral restraint, while the Jews had lived under the strict, isolating regime of the law.

Although these Jews had come to believe Jesus was the Christ, the Son of God, and had embraced Him in faith, it was hard for them to shake the restrictions of the Mosaic law. Their new-found liberty in Christ was hard to adjust to. It permitted them to eat and mix their foods as the Gentiles did, and gave them freedom from the celebrations of the feasts and the keeping of the sabbaths. However, old habits were hard to shake. Their conscience often troubled them. Were they really pleasing God by living in this liberty?

In fact, they wondered if their Gentile brethren were really living lives pleasing to God! Soon they found themselves judging the Gentiles' spirituality.

The Jews' questions and indecision were hard for the Gentile Christians to understand. They deemed the legalism of their Jewish brethren a weakness and began to regard them with contempt.

Aware of this divisive situation, Paul addressed in Romans 14 how the just are to live in relationship to one another and in relationship to the gray areas of Christian living.

Use the space below and write out the insights that you gleaned from Romans 14 regarding those weak in the faith (probably the Jews) and the others who understood their liberty (probably the Gentiles). This exercise will help you learn about both groups, and will also let you see Paul's instructions to each.

Those weak in the faith:

Those at liberty:

Now, Beloved, after all you've studied, what is your conclusion about drinking wine and/or strong drink? Write it out.

He's There, Woe to the Drunkard

Finally, let me share with you what I believe. My belief is based on Romans 14:21-23: "It is good not to eat meat or to drink wine, or to do anything by which your brother stumbles. The faith which you have, have as your own conviction before God. Happy is he who does not condemn himself in what he approves . . . whatever is not from faith is sin."

A Christian cannot drink wine unless he can do it with a clear conscience before God while at all times adhering to the clear teachings of God's Word. If a Christian does feel the liberty to drink wine, then he must be controlled by the law of love. His drinking should never cause another to stumble.

Although I would enjoy wine, I personally do not feel the liberty to drink it because I feel that I am to be an example among the believers. Therefore, wine and any other strong drink is not for me.

"Do not be deceived, God is not mocked; for whatever a man sows, this he will also reap. For the one who sows to his own flesh shall from the flesh reap corruption" (Galatians 6:7-8).

Not only will such a person reap corruption but he will also reap judgment. Woes are not reserved for the heathen only; a righteous God must judge sin wherever He finds it. Therefore, whoever seduces his neighbor to get him drunk on sin, that person shall someday drink the Lord's cup of wrath. What a warning this ought to be to those who are tempted to lead others into sin or into even the slightest compromise of God's Word.

We, as God's people, are not only to stay far away from sin and sinners who would entice us, but we are to be so like our God that we mourn over sin. In Ezekiel 9:3-4 we read that when God prepared to destroy Jerusalem, He called for a man clothed in linen with a writing case to "go through the midst of the city . . . and put a mark on the foreheads of the men who sigh and groan over all the abominations which are being committed in its midst." Then as the destroyers were sent forth, they were to "not touch any man on whom is the mark" (Ezekiel 9:6). But as to the wicked, God said, "My eye will have no pity nor shall I spare, but *I shall bring their conduct upon their heads*" (Ezekiel 9:10; emphasis added).

In view of this sober warning, my friends, may we seek to "save others, snatching them out of the fire; and on some have mercy with fear, hating even the garment polluted by the flesh. Now to Him who is able to keep you from stumbling, and to make you stand in the presence of His glory blameless with great joy . . . be glory, majesty, dominion, and authority" (Jude 23-25).

DAY SEVEN

The final woe in Habakkuk's taunt-song is against idolaters. As you read it, remember idolatry occurs when a person removes God from His rightful place of preeminence and puts something or someone else in that place. Habakkuk writes:

> What profit is the idol when its maker has carved it, or an image, a teacher of false-hood?
> For its maker trusts in his own handiwork
> When he fashions speechless idols.
> Woe to him who says to a piece of wood, "Awake!"
> To a dumb stone, "Arise!"
> And that is your teacher?
> Behold, it is overlaid with gold and silver,
> And there is no breath at all inside it
> (Habakkuk 2:18-19).

Idols may be symbolized or personified in a carved image of wood; a molded image of gold, silver, or some other material; or in a stick, stone, or some object of nature. The idols of America are not as easy to spot as the icons of Old Testament times or the fetishes of superstitious people who still worship other gods. Idols do not always take on some definitive form—especially in our day, age, and culture.

But never doubt it—they are just as real. They are just as damning.

It does seem ridiculous to worship something you have made with your own hands, doesn't it? And yet, aren't we equally as ridiculous when we listen to and worship the words and the works of other finite human beings while ignoring the living, inerrant Word of God?

I am always amazed at the audacity of men who sit in judgment on the truth of the Word of God, of those who seek to tell us that the Bible merely *contains* the Word of God. How can man be wise enough to tell us what parts of God's Word are from God and what parts are merely the invention of man's own will? I am floored by those who set themselves up as critics of the Old Testament, calling much of it myths or mere stories told to convey spiritual concepts.

Jesus said, "O foolish men and slow of heart to believe in all that the prophets have spoken!" (Luke 24:25). Did He not explain to the men on the road to Emmaus, "beginning with Moses and with all the prophets . . . the things concerning Himself in all the Scriptures"? (v. 27).

Our Lord never sought to correct, change, or add to God's Word. Instead, He confirmed its veracity over and over again. Do you think putting the reasoning of man, the writings of man, the wisdom of man, the psychology of man, the philosophy of man, the understanding of man, the experience of man, or the teaching of man above the Word of God might be considered idolatry?

Why is God against idolatry? Because its focus is on what man creates, rather than on the Creator. Because of this idolatry, man is ensnared by Satan, who is a murderer, liar and destroyer.

God loves us and desires our highest good. He made us for Himself. And His name is *Qanna*, which means "jealous." God is jealous for us. We tend to think of jealousy as something evil. Yet there is a good and proper jealousy. A husband or wife has every cause to be jealous if his or her mate is giving another their rightful affection and attention. And it is the same with God.

Nothing—no person or no object—is to take His rightful place in our affections or our attention. Think about it. Does He have the preeminence in your affections? Do you desire Him above all else and everyone else? Could you live without anyone but Him? Or have others—idols—crowded Him out so that you live for others above Him, seeking to please them above your God? And what priority do you give Him? How much of your attention does He receive? Do you talk with Him daily? Weekly? Monthly? Annually? Do you take vacations *from* God or *with* God?

Take a moment and think about these things. They are critical questions. Be objective. Write down any real or possible idols that keep God from His rightful place of preeminence in your life.

To have idols in your life is as great a sin as adultery or murder. To turn to alcohol to meet your needs or make you forget your problems is to make it an idol. Hear, oh, hear the word of the Lord in Exodus 20:3: "You shall have no other gods before Me." *Have you?* "You shall not worship them or serve them; for I, the LORD your God, am a jealous God, visiting the iniquity of the fathers on the children, on the third and the fourth generations of those who hate Me, but showing lovingkindness to thousands, to those who love Me and keep My commandments" (Exodus 20:5-6).

If there are idols in your life, how are others who watch you going to see "the LORD is in His holy temple"? (Habakkuk 2:20). Not only is His temple in heaven, but also in you. As part of the Church of Jesus Christ, you are His earthly temple. Clean God's temple; rid it of its idols. Let others see your uncompromising passion for Christ—and be silent before Him.

Note

1. Charles L. Feinberg, *The Minor Prophets* (Chicago: Moody Press, 1951), 212.

Chapter 10

HE'S THERE,
YOU CAN WALK
WITH HINDS' FEET

DAY ONE

One of the hardest situations for a Christian to handle is when a skeptic points out man's inhumanity toward man—and asks where God is.

If God is God—if He is so great, so almighty, so loving—where is He when a man strikes out in cruelty and hate at a fellow man? That is the skeptic's question—and before he'll even consider the gospel, he wants an answer. Period. End of argument!

What do you do? How do you answer?

Man's inhumanity to man *is* taking place all the time. Why *doesn't* God intervene?

The skeptic's problem is twofold. First, he sees evil triumph over good; and second, he doesn't see God intervening to stop it. If God is what the skeptic envisions, then He wouldn't allow that to happen. This is why he's a non-believer.

Skeptics don't understand that God allows such things even though He is sovereign and can intervene any time He wants. They have also missed the truth of God's just judgment. God will judge, and His judgment will be just.

Another matter skeptics don't understand—and you may not either, although you are not a skeptic—is that God is not ruled by love alone. God is also holy. He is other than man, different from man. He acts in accordance with the sum total of all His attributes, while man is often governed by his emotions, desires, and limited knowledge. Man is finite.

God sees all, knows all, and is eternal. One person's unbelief in God and His sovereignty does not change the fact that God is in control. He allows evil. He can intervene and many times He does, but only when it suits His eternal purpose.

If you are going to live in peace, you need to embrace in faith the reality that "the LORD is in His holy temple." Embrace it and be silent before Him. You don't need to argue. You don't need to defend God. Simply explain Him as the Word of God explains Him. Then it is the skeptic's responsibility to accept or reject the Word of God. The responsibility is his, not yours. It's between him and God. It's a matter of faith. Whom will he believe? His own reasoning? Man's arguments? Or God's Word?

Whether the skeptic believes or not—God is not going to move out of His temple. He remains God.

The skeptic can come into His temple through the cross of Jesus Christ and, in submission, bow the knee and confess that Jesus Christ is God. Or he can wait until hell and death give him up with the rest of the dead and he stands before God's great white throne to be judged according to his deeds which are written in the books. Then, before he is cast into the lake of fire where the worm dies not and the fire is not quenched, he will bow the knee and confess that Jesus Christ is God—to the glory of the Father.

He will be without excuse (Romans 1:20). He could have received the truth and understanding if he had embraced in faith the One Who said, "I am the way, and the truth, and the life; no one comes to the Father, but through Me" (John 14:6). The skeptic could have had the mind of Christ to understand these things (1 Corinthians 2:16); but instead, he chose to remain in the darkness of his own reasoning. In so doing, he chose death.

How sad. How very, very sad.

If you're like me, your spirit must be troubled at not only the blindness of men but also at all that is going on in our world. I want so badly to do something about all of the corruption. I long to air our television program on prime-time television and open up God's Word under His anointing and let people know where we're headed if we don't repent. Oh, that someone could be heard who would at least put the holy fear of God into people so they would think twice before they blatantly, needlessly rush headlong into iniquity and eventual destruction!

If you know God's Word, and don't have your head buried in the sand of your own little world, then I am sure you can understand and relate to my frustration. What can we—you and I—do?

This is what Habakkuk was asking. He knew what was going on, and it frustrated him. His recourse is ours: God.

We must lay our questions, frustrations, anxieties, and impotence at the feet of God and wait for His answer. And then receiving it, we must live by faith.

God assured Habakkuk that the ungodly would not go unpunished—woes were determined, and would not fail. But knowledge of coming judgment is not enough. There is one more thing we need to be assured of (and it is this that keeps me plodding along in the place of my appointment):

This truth is God's final reassuring word to Habakkuk. The world may be worshiping idols, justice may be perverted, wickedness may abound, strife and violence may be the order of the day . . . but God is not like the idols who cannot speak. God is in His holy temple. He has pronounced His woes. Sin will be judged. His judgment will come. It will not fail. Let all the earth hush. They have no rebuttal, no excuse, no justified complaint, nothing to say to God. The wisdom and cleverness of man has failed. Man's impotence is obvious, his judgment sure.

God is God—immutable, eternal. All is under His control. What He has planned for Israel and for the Church will come to pass. Keep silent, O world.

And you, child of God, live by your faith. You can. Faith will hold, because it is faith in the everlasting Sovereign Ruler of all the universe, the Creator of heaven and earth, the One Who sits on *the throne.* He's in His holy temple.

I do not know your trials or your frustrations. I cannot know what might be troubling you or making you anxious. But God knows those things. What you do not understand, what you feel unable to cope with, can be overcome moment by moment if you will live by faith and walk in communion with Him.

In Habakkuk 3, we have the "prayer of Habakkuk

the prophet, according to Shigionoth" (3:1). We also come across the word *Selah* in verses 3, 9, and 13. Although no one seems to be certain about the precise meaning of these terms, let's take a few minutes to look at what I have gleaned from others regarding the meaning of *Shigionoth* and *Selah*.

The singular term for Shigionoth, *Shiggaion*, is used in the introduction of Psalm 7. According to the footnote in the New American Standard Bible, a Shigionoth is "dithyrambic rhythm or a wild, passionate song." Others say it refers to the kind of music which accompanied the song. Since the word comes from a verb meaning "to err," the thought is one of a song sung in great excitement, a triumphal song.[1]

Selah, which occurs seventy times in the Psalms and three times in this chapter, indicates a heightening of the musical accompaniment, the musical forte. As you have seen earlier in this study, it would allow for a pause and meditation.[2]

Now, stop and read the third chapter of Habakkuk in the back of this book. In the margin, note the four paragraph divisions of the chapter (at verses 2,3,8,16), and record the theme of each paragraph in the right-hand margin.

After reading Habakkuk 3, can you see why this is a prayer according to Shigionoth? The Lord will come for the salvation of His people.

You needn't cry out, "Lord, where are you?" He's in His holy temple. Be silent, hush—it is all right. You, like Habakkuk, can have hinds' feet on high places. Sing your prayer of triumph, your Shigionoth, Beloved.

Selah.

Habakkuk finally saw beyond the immediate circumstances troubling him and realized that although God was going to use the godless Babylonians, *there was a purpose in what God was doing. He was fulfilling His sovereign plan—for Israel and for the nations.*

Israel would be judged through the Babylonian invasion and captivity, but that was not to be the end of Israel. God would revive His work in the midst of the years. In wrath He remembers mercy, because like Himself, His ways are everlasting.

As He did before, God will come from Teman; He will go forth for the salvation of His anointed as He marches in indignation through the earth and tramples the nations (Habakkuk 3:2-3,6,13).

Although the present and the near future looked bleak, it was only temporary. God's promises for Israel would stand. Nothing could ever change them. They would not fail. Habakkuk's God was the everlasting One Who does not change, but keeps His covenants.

I believe Habakkuk's prophetic prayer gives us a glimpse beyond the coming judgment of the Babylonians and their destruction to the judgment of the nations and Israel's ultimate survival.

Many Bible commentators do not see this as referring to the second coming of Christ. Some believe it looks back at God's deliverance of His people from the land of Egypt, others at the Babylonian invasion.

However, since we are living on the brink of God's final judgment when His righteous wrath will be poured out on the world, I want us to take a look at the second coming of our Lord. As we peer more deeply into the content of the prophet's prayer, I want us also to compare this passage with other scriptures about our Lord's second coming.

Christians are usually unanimous in the fact that Christ is coming again. It is on details concerning the timing, the state of the Church, and Israel's status during this period on which we differ.

In order to prepare you for a look at the final coming of our Lord, let me give you an assignment.

1. Read through Romans 11 carefully. It is printed out here for you.

2. Depending on how much time you have available for this devotional study, go through Romans 11 and mark every reference to the Gentiles in one way and every reference to the Jews in another. You can pick up the references to the Jews by marking words such as "His people," "Israel," "natural branches," and of course, the pronouns which relate to these words. The Gentiles are sometimes called "wild olives."

3. Mark every reference to God.

ROMANS 11

I say then, God has not rejected His people, has He? May it never be! For I too am an Israelite, a descendant of Abraham, of the tribe of Benjamin. God has not rejected His people whom He foreknew. Or do you not know what the Scripture says in the passage about Elijah, how he pleads with God against Israel? "Lord, THEY HAVE KILLED THY PROPHETS, THEY HAVE TORN DOWN THINE ALTARS, AND I ALONE AM LEFT, AND THEY ARE SEEKING MY LIFE." But what is the divine response to him? "I HAVE KEPT for Myself SEVEN THOUSAND MEN WHO HAVE NOT BOWED THE KNEE TO BAAL." In the same way then, there has also come to be at the present time a remnant according to God's gracious choice. But if it is by grace, it is no longer on the basis of works, otherwise grace is no longer grace. What then? That which Israel is seeking for, it has not obtained, but those who were chosen obtained it, and the rest were hardened; just as it is written,

"God gave them a spirit of stupor,
Eyes to see not and ears to hear not,
Down to this very day."
And David says,
"Let their table become a snare and a trap,
And a stumbling block and a retribution to them.
Let their eyes be darkened to see not,
And bend their backs forever."

I say then, they did not stumble so as to fall, did they? May it never be! But by their transgression salvation has come to the Gentiles, to make them jealous. Now if their transgression be riches for the world and their failure be riches for the Gentiles, how much more will their fulfillment be! But I am speaking to you who are Gentiles. Inasmuch then as I am an apostle of Gentiles, I magnify my ministry, if somehow I might move to jealousy my fellow countrymen and save some of them. For if their rejection be the reconciliation of the world, what will their acceptance be but life from the dead? And if the first piece of dough be holy, the lump is also; and if the root be holy, the branches are too. But if some of the branches were broken off, and you, being a wild olive, were grafted in among them and became partaker with them of the rich root of the olive tree, do not be arrogant toward the branches; but if you are arrogant, remember that it is not you who supports the root, but the root supports you. You will say then, "Branches were broken off so that I might be grafted in." Quite right, they were broken off for their unbelief, but you stand by your faith. Do not be conceited, but fear; for if God did not spare the natural branches, neither will He spare you. Behold then the kindness and severity of God; to those who fell, severity, but to you, God's kindness, if you continue in His kindness; otherwise you also will be cut off. And they also, if they do not continue in their unbelief, will be grafted in; for God is able to graft them in again. For if you were cut off from what is by nature a wild olive tree, and were grafted contrary to nature into a cultivated olive tree, how much more shall these who are the natural branches be grafted into their own olive tree? For I do not want you, brethren, to be uninformed of this mystery, lest you be wise in your own estimation, that a partial hardening has happened to Israel until the fulness of the Gentiles has come in; and thus all Israel will be saved; just as it is written,

"THE DELIVERER WILL COME FROM ZION,
HE WILL REMOVE UNGODLINESS FROM JACOB."
"AND THIS IS MY COVENANT WITH THEM,
WHEN I TAKE AWAY THEIR SINS."

From the standpoint of the gospel they are enemies for your sake, but from the standpoint of God's choice they are beloved for the sake of the fathers; for the gifts and the calling of God are irrevocable. For just as you once were disobedient to God, but now have been shown mercy because of their disobedience, so these also now have been disobedient, in order that because of the mercy shown to you they also may now be shown mercy. For God has shut up all in disobedience that He might show mercy to all.

Oh, the depth of the riches both of the wisdom and knowledge of God! How unsearchable are His judgments and unfathomable His ways! FOR

WHO HAS KNOWN THE MIND OF THE LORD, OR WHO
BECAME HIS COUNSELOR? OR WHO HAS FIRST GIVEN
TO HIM THAT IT MIGHT BE PAID BACK TO HIM AGAIN?
For from Him and through Him and to Him are
all things. To Him be the glory forever. Amen.

4. Now, Beloved, I want you to do an assignment
that will benefit and bless you greatly. List everything
you learn about the Jews, the Gentiles, and God from
this chapter.

The Jews:

The Gentiles:

God:

DAY THREE

God is through with the Jews.

That is a statement I hear in some theological circles. Often the people who say it believe that the Church is now the seed of Abraham and, therefore, God is finished dealing with Israel as a nation.

Granted, "if you belong to Christ, then you are Abraham's offspring, heirs according to promise" (Galatians 3:29), for the "Scripture, foreseeing that God would justify the Gentiles by faith, preached the gospel beforehand to Abraham, saying, 'ALL THE NATIONS SHALL BE BLESSED IN YOU.' So then those who are of faith are blessed with Abraham, the believer" (vv. 8-9).

But does this mean God is through with the nation of Israel?

When I look at the teaching of the Word of God as a whole, it seems obvious God is not finished with Israel.

Let's return to Romans 11 now and do a little more study on this subject, for I believe it will determine how you might interpret Habakkuk 3.

1. A metaphor is an implied comparison between two things. It is a figure of speech in which a word or a phrase that usually means one thing is used to describe something else in order for you to see a comparison or likeness between two unlike things. What metaphor or metaphors are used for Israel and for the Gentiles in Romans 11?

2. According to Romans 11, what is the ultimate future of Israel? When will it happen? As I ask that last

question, I am not referring to the date of its happening, but rather to the event that first must take place, according to Romans 11.

3. Draw a picture, sketching out what God is saying in respect to the olive tree and its branches. It will help crystallize what this chapter is teaching.

Don't you stand in awe of God and of His ways? Doesn't it give you great confidence to know that the gifts and the calling of God are irrevocable? God's dealings with Israel, His patience and persistence, His lovingkindnesses, His fulfillment of His Word, all testify to the fact that He will act in the same consistent way with you. Think about it. It should bring you peace even as it did Habakkuk when he couldn't understand what God was doing.

As you studied Romans 11, did you have a difficult time understanding why God would do all of this and how He is going to do it? Then in a way, your questions are similar to Habakkuk's.

Listen to Jeremiah 23:3-8:

Then I Myself shall gather the remnant of My flock out of all the countries where I have driven them and shall bring them back to their pasture;

and they will be fruitful and multiply. I shall also raise up shepherds over them and they will tend them; and they will not be afraid any longer, nor be terrified, nor will any be missing," declares the LORD.

"Behold, the days are coming," declares the
    LORD,
"When I shall raise up for David a righteous
    Branch;
And He will reign as king and act wisely
And do justice and righteousness in the land.
In His days Judah will be saved,
And Israel will dwell securely;
And this is His name by which He will be
    called,
'The LORD our righteousness.'

"Therefore behold, the days are coming," declares the LORD, "when they will no longer say, 'As the LORD lives, who brought up the sons of Israel from the land of Egypt,' but, 'As the Lord lives, who brought up and led back the descendants of the household of Israel from the north land and from all the countries where I had driven them.'" Then they will live on their own soil.

1. Remember that Jeremiah was present and prophesying during Babylon's siege of Jerusalem. In this passage, Jeremiah is giving the people hope. How?

2. Who is the righteous Branch raised up for David? I believe it's a prophecy regarding our Lord Jesus Christ.

a. What do you learn from this prophecy regarding Israel's future?

b. Do you see any relationship to the promise in Jeremiah and Romans 11? What, if any?

3. Reread Romans 11:33-36, and write out what you think Paul is saying in these verses.

4. Do you see any parallel between Romans 11:33-36 and Habakkuk 3:16-19? Write it out.

Do you remember the passage below? We read it in week four as we looked at our covenant-keeping God.

Thus says the LORD,
Who gives the sun for light by day,
And fixed order of the moon
    and the stars for light by night,
Who stirs up the sea so that its waves roar;
The LORD of hosts is His name:
"If this fixed order departs
From before Me," declares the LORD,
"Then the offspring of Israel also shall cease
From being a nation before Me forever."

Thus says the LORD,
"If the heavens above can be measured,
And the foundations of the earth searched out
     below,
Then I wil also cast off all the offspring of
     Israel
For all that they have done," declares the LORD.

"Behold, days are coming," declares the LORD,
"when the city shall be rebuilt for the LORD
from the Tower of Hananel to the Corner Gate.
And the measuring line shall go out farther
straight ahead to the hill Gareb; then it will
turn to Goah. And the whole valley of the dead
bodies and of thc ashes, and all the fields as far
as the brook Kidron, to the corner of the Horse
Gate toward the east, shall be holy to the LORD;
it shall not be plucked up, or overthrown anymore forever (Jeremiah 31:35-40).

Beloved, I cannot see that God's Word teaches He
is finished with Israel. Continuing through the
Scripture, we read this:

Now the LORD saw,
And it was displeasing in His sight
     that there was no justice.
And He saw that there was no man,
And was astonished that there was no one to
     intercede;
Then His own arm brought salvation to Him;
And His righteousness upheld Him.
And He put on righteousness like a breastplate,
And a helmet of salvation on His head;
And He put on garments of vengeance for
     clothing,
And wrapped Himself with zeal as a mantle.
According to their deeds, so He will repay,
Wrath to His adversaries, recompense to His
     enemies;
To the coastlands He will make recompense.

So they will fear the name of the LORD from the
     west
And His glory from the rising of the sun,
For He will come like a rushing stream,
Which the wind of the LORD drives.
"And a Redeemer will come to Zion,
And to those who turn from transgression in
     Jacob,"
declares the LORD.
"And as for Me, this is My covenant with them,"
says the LORD: "My Spirit which is upon you,
and My words which I have put in your mouth,
shall not depart from your mouth, nor from the
mouth of your offspring, nor from the mouth of
your offspring's offspring," says the LORD, "from
now and forever" (Isaiah 59:15b-21).

DAY FOUR

A prayer of Habakkuk the prophet, according
     to Shigionoth.
LORD, I have heard the report about Thee and I
     fear.
O LORD, revive Thy work in the midst of the
     years,
In the midst of the years make it known;
In wrath remember mercy (Habakkuk 3:1-2).

Once Habakkuk understood what God was going
to do, he seemed to urge God to move ahead with
His plans.

When the prophet had a clear understanding of
what God planned to do about Judah's sin and the
judgment of the people whom He would use as His
instrument, Habakkuk said, "Revive Thy work in the
midst of the years, in the midst of the years make it
known."

Once you understand that God judges wickedness,
that He will bring it to a halt, and that He will exalt
righteousness and vindicates the righteous, aren't you

anxious to have God get on with His plans? I want wickedness to be stopped. I hate what man is doing to man. It burdens me that the innocent suffer because of the ungodly deeds of a perverse generation.

As I sat and talked with a young mother the other day, we discussed how crucial it is these days to watch our children virtually every minute we are out in public. Why? Because there are so many people stealing children right out from under parents' eyes.

Not too long ago a family we know went to Disney World with their two children. One was in a stroller, the other walking beside Mommy and Daddy. Suddenly she was missing. They panicked.

As they went for help, the police at Disney World told them to split up and go stand at two different exits while they closed all the other exits. As they stood at the gates, they were told to carefully look straight into the eyes of each child leaving the park.

Time passed, seeming to drag on into eternity, but they obeyed the police and looked carefully into the eyes of each child. Finally a couple approached the gate with their weary child asleep on the father's shoulder. The child was covered with a blanket. The parents of the sleeping child seemed unperturbed when they were asked to pull back the blanket so they could view the child.

As the child was nudged and awakened, they looked into her drowsy, sleepy eyes. The parent of the lost little girl knew they had found their child. The clothes were not the same. Their daughter was dressed as a boy. Her pretty hair was gone. It had been cut like a boy's and even dyed another color, but the child was theirs.

I remember the freedom of my childhood, playing unattended outside, walking to the corner store. The young mother I talked with remembers being dropped off at the mall for a few hours. But today many parents don't allow their children to enter a public restroom unattended. When Jack and I take our grandchildren out, they never leave their Mimi or Pa's side.

How we long for God to revive His work! We want men to again fear God and tremble before Him. We want our Lord to hurry and come, for even though it means judgment to the wicked, it will bring salvation to the righteous.

Oh, my friend, are you in pain? Hurting and confused? His coming will bring all that to an end. God's own hand will wipe away all of your tears. Justice will reign supreme. So pray for the peace of Jerusalem—for the Deliverer to come out of Zion.

He has said, "Yes, I am coming quickly." May your prayer and mine be, "Amen. Come, Lord Jesus" (Revelation 22:20).

DAY FIVE

"In wrath remember mercy" (Habakkuk 3:2). This is Habakkuk's cry as he hears of God's coming judgment.

At God's bidding, the Babylonians would sweep down upon them. Habakkuk could not help but fear. Weakness entered his bones, and he trembled because he "must wait quietly for the days of distress, for the people to arise who will invade [them]" (Habakkuk 3:16). And yet, as we have just seen, he *wanted* this day of distress to come for sometime after that day the Lord would come for the salvation of His people. The Babylonians—and eventually every other wicked nation—would be threshed or trampled by God (3:12-13). Therefore, Habakkuk prayed, "O LORD, revive Thy work in the midst of the years, in the midst of the years make it known" (3:2).

In Habakkuk 3 we behold the kindness and severity of God (Romans 11:22)—severity in judging sin, kindness in redeeming His chosen people. Habakkuk, looking beyond the just but severe wrath of God, awaited His coming for the salvation of His own. Although some feel God is through with Israel because of their rejection of the gospel, this is what God's Word teaches us:

A partial hardening [against the gospel] has happened to Israel until the fulness of the Gentiles has come in; and thus all Israel will be saved; just as it is written,
"THE DELIVERER WILL COME FROM ZION [a reference to the heavenly Zion],
HE WILL REMOVE UNGODLINESS FROM JACOB."
"AND THIS IS MY COVENANT WITH THEM,
WHEN I TAKE AWAY THEIR SINS"
(Romans 11:25-27).

The Deliverer Who is to come from Zion is the same deliverer Habakkuk describes in 3:3-15. He is the same One referred to in Jeremiah as "the righteous Branch." He is the "Son of Man" referred to in Daniel 7:13-14:

I kept looking in the night visions, and behold, with the clouds of heaven one like a Son of Man was coming, and He came up to the Ancient of Days and was presented before Him. And to Him was given dominion, glory and a kingdom that all the peoples, nations, and men of every language might serve Him. His dominion is an everlasting dominion which will not pass away; and His kingdom is one which will not be destroyed.

Habakkuk awaited the deliverance of God, remembering God's deliverance in the past when He brought them out of Egypt, took them through the wilderness, and brought them into the land of Canaan. He remembered when God caused the sun to stand still so that Joshua could win his battle. The One Who mightily delivered in the past, judging Israel's enemies in His wake, was the same One Who would deliver them again . . . and again until all was in subjection under His feet.

Understanding that Habakkuk was looking at God from the perspective of His past deliverances, I want us to look at how this parallels our Lord's final coming.

When you are familiar with the prophetic passages of Scripture, you can see the similarities between Habakkuk 3:3-15 and the second coming of Jesus Christ. Let's look at a few. Look up each reference and write out what you see in each one.

Habakkuk 3:3-4   Matthew 24:27

Habakkuk 3:5   Revelation 6 (the result of breaking the seals in Revelation 5)

Habakkuk 3:6,9   Zechariah 14:3-5,8

Habakkuk 3:11   Zechariah 14:6-7

Matthew 24:29

Habakkuk 3:12   Revelation 14:14-20;19:15
                                 Isaiah 63:1-6

Habakkuk 3:13-14   Revelation 19:17-21

This, Beloved, is what it will be like when the Lord Jesus Christ comes a second time—going forth for the salvation of Israel, remembering His covenant.

I wonder how long it will be before He comes? Will you be ready? Meditate on these words from Revelation 22:10-15. As you do, remember that Daniel's prophecy regarding the last days preceding the setting up of God's kingdom on earth was sealed to Daniel so he couldn't understand it. However, when Revelation, which parallels much with Daniel, was written, it was not sealed—it could be understood!

> And he said to me, "Do not seal up the words of the prophecy of this book, for the time is near. Let the one who does wrong, still do wrong; and let the one who is filthy, still be filthy; and let the one who is righteous, still

219

practice righteousness; and let the one who is holy, still keep himself holy.

"Behold, I am coming quickly, and My reward is with Me, to render to every man according to what he has done. I am the Alpha and the Omega, the first and the last, the beginning and the end."

Blessed are those who wash their robes, that they may have the right to the tree of life, and may enter by the gates into the city. Outside are the dogs and the sorcerers and the immoral persons and the murderers and the idolaters, and everyone who loves and practices lying.

Oh Father, in wrath remember mercy.

DAY SIX

When God does not seem to answer you or move on your behalf—when you cannot seem to go on—what do you do?

You **remember that your times are in His hands**. This, Beloved, is the fourth major truth you need to keep before you. This is what sustained Habakkuk, and it is what will sustain you when there seems no relief in sight and when you are weak and weary of fighting the good fight, of running the race with endurance.

As we read those last magnificent and unparalleled words of faith in Habakkuk 3:16-19, we see that Habakkuk has contented himself with God's timetable. He states, "I must wait quietly for the day of distress, for the people to arise who will invade us" (3:16). The Lord was in His holy temple and Habakkuk could be silent. He could wait quietly. Habakkuk's resignation was not one of defeat but of faith. He went on to say that he would rejoice in the God of *his* salvation.

God does not want compliant resignation. When life is difficult, God wants us to have a faith that trusts and waits. He wants us to have a faith that does not complain while waiting, but rejoices because we know our times are in His hands—nail-scarred hands that labor for our highest good.

Corrie Ten Boom was a single woman who ended up in Hitler's extermination camps because she and her family hid Jews in their home in Holland during World War II. Her release from that camp was a miracle only to be followed by another—her worldwide ministry.

At the age of ninety-one, five years before her death, our sovereign Father allowed Corrie to have a stroke which left her speechless. Pam, the woman who cared for Corrie, wrote discussing "why God had allowed this illness to take place. We wondered, talked, and prayed on the subject, but never came up with a complete answer to the mystery. We felt there was a lot we did not understand about why God allows suffering. What came to us in increasing measure was an assurance of the absolute sovereignty of God.

"Of vital importance to me was the growing realization that our times were completely in God's hands. He knew the length of Tante Corrie's life. It did not depend on anything except His will." Corrie's daily prayer was: "Lord, keep me close to Your heart so that I see things as it were more and more from Your point of view." 3

This, Beloved, is my prayer for you and for me as we joyfully surrender in faith to the truth that our times are in His hands. In doing so, I know we will find Him to be our strength even as He was Corrie's.

> But as for me, I trust in Thee, O LORD,
> I say, "Thou art my God."
> My times are in Thy hand;
> Deliver me from the hand of my enemies, and
> from those who persecute me.
> Make Thy face to shine upon Thy servant;
> Save me in Thy lovingkindness.
> Let me not be put to shame, O LORD, for I call
> upon Thee;
> Let the wicked be put to shame,
> let them be silent in Sheol.
> Let the lying lips be dumb,
> Which speak arrogantly against the righteous
> With pride and contempt.
>
> How great is Thy goodness,
> Which Thou hast stored up for those who fear
> Thee,
> Which Thou hast wrought for those who take
> refuge in Thee,
> Before the sons of men!

Thou dost hide them in the secret place of Thy
    presence from the conspiracies of man;
Thou dost keep them secretly in a shelter from
    the strife of tongues.
Blessed be the LORD,
For He has made marvelous His lovingkindness
    to me in a besieged city.
As for me, I said in my alarm,
"I am cut off from before Thine eyes";
Nevertheless Thou didst hear the voice of my
supplications
When I cried to Thee.

O love the LORD, all you His godly ones!
The LORD preserves the faithful, and fully
    recompenses the proud doer.
Be strong, and let your heart take courage,
All you who hope in the Lord (Psalm 31:14-24).

Oh, dear one, when you doubt, when iniquity
abounds, when you want to question God, there are
two things you need to do. First, run immediately into
the ever-open arms of your Father. You have wel-
come access to the arms of your omnipotent,
sovereign God, so do not look to the arm of flesh. In
faith, fling yourself into all that He is, into all that He
has said.

Second, rejoice in Him. In a sense, rejoicing acti-
vates your faith, for you are saying, "Father, You are all
that I need. You are the One in Whom I will trust
'though the fig tree should not blossom, and there be
no fruit on the vines, though the yield of the olive
should fail, and the fields produce no food, though the
flock should be cut off from the fold, and there be no
cattle in the stalls'" (Habakkuk 3:17).

When you fling yourself in faith into all God is and
all His Word says, when you rejoice in Him in the face
of every circumstance, then you will know His strength.
It is a strength that will enable you to walk with hinds'

feet on high places. Hinds' feet do not slip. Isn't that wonderful! It is most often at the difficult times when Christians stumble. They turn to the arm of flesh, something or someone other than God, and in the process, turn from Him. And the arm of flesh is not the answer.

Remember in week seven when we looked at Jeremiah 17:5-8?

> Cursed is the man who trusts in mankind
> And makes flesh his strength,
> And whose heart turns away from the LORD.
> For he will be like a bush in the desert
> And will not see when prosperity comes,
> But will live in stony wastes in the
> wilderness" (vv. 5-6)

A person who does not cling to God's Word in faith will find his life dry and barren. But . . .

> Blessed is the man who trusts in the LORD
> And whose trust is the LORD.
> For he will be like a tree planted by the water,
> That extends its roots by a stream
> And will not fear when the heat comes;
> But its leaves will be green,
> And it will not be anxious in a year of drought
> Nor cease to yield fruit (vv. 7-8).

What is God saying to us in Jeremiah? He wants us to see the same thing that Habakkuk saw. Though difficulties, trials, and testings come, though temporal blessings fail, we can overcome if we will cling to God in faith. He is our strength. You and I can have green leaves in drought time and bear fruit if our roots run deep in faith.

Precious friend, when you find yourself in difficult and trying situations, do not be proud and try to handle life in your own strength. Live by faith. Exult in the Lord; rejoice in the God of your salvation. He is able to deliver you from—and through—any difficulty of life.

He will be your strength and give you hinds' feet on high places.

Selah, Beloved, Selah.

DAY SEVEN

The fifth and final truth to brand on your heart is this: **Fear and doubt are conquered by a faith that rejoices**.

Praise is the sparkplug of faith. Praise gets faith airborne where it can soar above the gravitational forces of this world's cares. The secret of faith is continual praise—even when your inward parts tremble, your lips quiver, and decay enters your bones.

When Corrie Ten Boom and her sister Betsy were taken to a German concentration camp, they were ordered to strip naked and pass before the watching eyes of German soldiers. To some women today, this would not mean a thing, but to these two godly women who had been sheltered in the purity of a home where Christ was honored without compromise, this was a horrifying experience. Not only were they enduring great humiliation, they also did not know what awaited them. There was the terror of the unknown, for they knew they were considered enemies.

How did they endure? How did they keep from totally losing their inner peace as they stood naked before eyes filled with curiosity, anger, or blatant lust? Betsy turned to Corrie and told her that they were going to rejoice in the fellowship of His sufferings, for Jesus, too, had been stripped naked and exposed to the eyes of men at Calvary.

And rejoice they did—time and time again. Oh, not because there was something to rejoice about, but because there was Someone in Whom they could rejoice! Their fear and doubt were conquered by a faith that enabled them to rejoice—no matter what their circumstances or their future.

They did what Habakkuk did. Listen to his words: "Yet I will exult in the LORD, I will rejoice in the God of my salvation" (3:18).

I know, Beloved, that it is not easy to rejoice when you find yourself in the midst of devastating circumstances. To rejoice in such circumstances seems like insanity. But it is not in circumstances that you are to rejoice, but in the God Who is in charge of the circumstances! With the apostle Paul, you can say, "Not that I speak from want; for I have learned to be content in whatever circumstances I am. I know how to get along with humble means, and I also know how to live in prosperity; in any and every circumstance I have learned the secret of being filled and going hungry, both of having abundance and suffering need. I can do all things through Him who strengthens me" (Philippians 4:11-13). God is fully adequate.

In your trial, this is what you need to remember:

God is in control. He is in charge of history, because He is sovereign.

History centers on the Jewish people and the children of God.

There is a purpose in what God is doing, whether or not you see or understand it.

Your times are in His hands.

And your fear and doubt will be conquered by a faith which rejoices.

We can rejoice in our circumstances because we are not looking at them, but at Him. Oh, Beloved, your faith will become airborne when you "consider it all joy . . . when you encounter various trials" and when in faith you are "always giving thanks for all things" (James 1:2, Ephesians 5:20). Truly, this is how "the righteous will live by his faith" and, in doing so, he will discover that "the Lord GOD is my strength, and He has made my feet like hinds' feet, and makes me walk on my high places" (Habakkuk 2:4; 3:19).

Habakkuk's days were draped in darkness, just as yours may be. But the darkness did not overwhelm him! In faith he pulled back the curtains and saw the rising Son, coming in glory to dispel the dark night of the soul.

Where is God when bad things happen? He's behind the curtains, directing, and overseeing it all. Walk with hinds' feet on faith's mountaintops!

Notes

1. Feinberg, 216.
2. Feinberg, 217.
3. Pamela Rosewell, *The Five Silent Years of Corrie Ten Boom* (Grand Rapids, Mich. Zondervan Books, 1986), 85.

THE BOOK OF HABAKKUK

CHAPTER ONE

The oracle which Habakkuk the prophet saw.

How long, O LORD, will I call for help,
And Thou wilt not hear?
I cry out to Thee, "Violence!"
Yet Thou dost not save.
Why dost Thou make me see iniquity,
And cause me to look on wickedness?
Yes, destruction and violence are before me;
Strife exists and contention arises.
Therefore, the law is ignored

And justice is never upheld.
For the wicked surround the righteous;
Therefore, justice comes out perverted.

"Look among the nations! Observe!
Be astonished! Wonder!
Because I am doing something in your days—
You would not believe if you were told.
"For behold, I am raising up the Chaldeans,
That fierce and impetuous people
Who march throughout the earth
To seize dwelling places which are not theirs.
"They are dreaded and feared.
Their justice and authority originate with them-
    selves.
"Their horses are swifter than leopards
And keener than wolves in the evening.
Their horsemen come galloping,
Their horsemen come from afar;
They fly like an eagle swooping down to
    devour.
"All of them come for violence.
Their horde of faces moves forward.
They collect captives like sand.
"They mock at kings,
And rulers are a laughing matter to them.
They laugh at every fortress,
And heap up rubble to capture it.
"Then they will sweep through like the wind
    and pass on.
But they will be held guilty,
They whose strength is their god."

Art Thou not from everlasting,
O LORD, my God, my Holy One?
We will not die.
Thou, O LORD, hast appointed them to judge;
And Thou, O Rock, hast established them to
    correct.
Thine eyes are too pure to approve evil,

And Thou canst not look on wickedness with
favor.
Why dost Thou look with favor
On those who deal treacherously?
Why art Thou silent when the wicked swallow
up
Those more righteous than they?
Why hast Thou made men like the fish of the
sea,
Like creeping things without a ruler over them?
The Chaldeans bring all of them up with a
hook,
Drag them away with their net,
And gather them together in their fishing net.
Therefore, they rejoice and are glad.
Therefore, they offer a sacrifice to their net.
And burn incense to their fishing net;
Because through these things their catch is
large,
And their food is plentiful.
Will they therefore empty their net
And continually slay nations without sparing?

<h2 style="text-align:center">CHAPTER TWO</h2>

I will stand on my guard post
And station myself on the rampart;
And I will keep watch to see what He will
speak to me,
And how I may reply when I am reproved.
Then the LORD answered me and said,
"Record the vision
And inscribe it on tablets,
That the one who reads it may run.
For the vision is yet for the appointed time;
It hastens toward the goal, and it will not fail.
Though it tarries, wait for it;
For it will certainly come, it will not delay.

"Behold, as for the proud one,
His soul is not right within him;
But the righteous will live by his faith.
Furthermore, wine betrays the haughty man,
So that he does not stay at home.
He enlarges his appetite like Sheol,
And he is like death, never satisfied.
He also gathers to himself all nations
And collects to himself all peoples.
Will not all of these take up a taunt-song
    against him,
Even mockery and insinuations against him,
And say, 'Woe to him who increases what is
    not his—
For how long—
And makes himself rich with loans?'
Will not your creditors rise up suddenly,
And those who collect from you awaken?
Indeed, you will become plunder for them.
Because you have looted many nations,
All the remainder of the peoples will loot
    you—
Because of human bloodshed and violence
    done to the land,
To the town and all its inhabitants.

"Woe to him who gets evil gain for his house
To put his nest on high
To be delivered from the hand of calamity!
You have devised a shameful thing for your
    house
By cutting off many peoples;
So you are sinning against yourself.
Surely the stone will cry out from the wall,
And the rafter will answer it from the frame-
    work.

"Woe to him who builds a city with bloodshed
And founds a town with violence!
Is it not indeed from the LORD of hosts

That peoples toil for fire,
And nations grow weary for nothing?
For the earth will be filled
With the knowledge of the glory of the LORD,
As the waters cover the sea.

"Woe to you who make your neighbors drink,
Who mix in your venom even to make them
    drunk
So as to look on their nakedness!
You will be filled with disgrace rather than
    honor.
Now you yourself drink and expose your own
    nakedness.
The cup in the LORD's right hand will come
    around to you,
And utter disgrace will come upon your glory.
For the violence done to Lebanon will over-
    whelm you,
And the devastation of its beasts by which you
terrified them,
Because of human bloodshed and violence
    done to the land,
To the town and all its inhabitants.

"What profit is the idol when its maker has
    carved it,
Or an image, a teacher of falsehood?
For its maker trusts in his own handiwork
When he fashions speechless idols.
Woe to him who says to a piece of wood,
    'Awake!'
To a dumb stone, 'Arise!'
And that is your teacher?
Behold, it is overlaid with gold and silver,
And there is no breath at all inside it.
But the LORD is in His holy temple.
Let all the earth be silent before Him."

CHAPTER THREE

A prayer of Habakkuk the prophet, according
to Shigionoth.

LORD, I have heard the report about Thee and I
fear.
O LORD, revive Thy work in the midst of the
years,
In the midst of the years make it known;
In wrath remember mercy.

God comes from Teman,
And the Holy One from Mount Paran. Selah.
His splendor covers the heavens,
And the earth is full of His praise.
His radiance is like the sunlight;
He has rays flashing from His hand,
And there is the hiding of His power.
Before Him goes pestilence,
And plague comes after Him.
He stood and surveyed the earth;
He looked and startled the nations.
Yes, the perpetual mountains were shattered,
The ancient hills collapsed.
His ways are everlasting.
I saw the tents of Cushan under distress,
The tent curtains of the land of Midian were
trembling.

Did the LORD rage against the rivers,
Or was Thine anger against the rivers,
Or was Thy wrath against the sea,
That Thou didst ride on Thy horses,
On Thy chariots of salvation?
Thy bow was made bare,
The rods of chastisement were sworn. Selah.
Thou didst cleave the earth with rivers.
The mountains saw Thee and quaked;
The downpour of waters swept by.
The deep uttered forth its voice,

It lifted high its hands.
Sun and moon stood in their places;
They went away at the light of Thine arrows,
At the radiance of Thy gleaming spear.
In indignation Thou didst march through the
  earth;
In anger Thou didst trample the nations.
Thou didst go forth for the salvation of Thy
  people,
For the salvation of Thine anointed.
Thou didst strike the head of the house of the
  evil
To lay him open from thigh to neck. Selah.
Thou didst pierce with his own spears
The head of his throngs.
They stormed in to scatter us;
Their exultation was like those
Who devour the oppressed in secret.
Thou didst tread on the sea with Thy horses,
On the surge of many waters.

I heard and my inward parts trembled,
At the sound my lips quivered.
Decay enters my bones,
And in my place I tremble.
Because I must wait quietly for the day of dis-
  tress,
For the people to arise who will invade us.
Though the fig tree should not blossom,
And there be no fruit on the vines,
Though the yield of the olive should fail,
And the fields produce no food,
Though the flock should be cut off from the
  fold,
And there be no cattle in the stalls,
Yet I will exult in the LORD,
I will rejoice in the God of my salvation.
The Lord GOD is my strength,
And He has made my feet like hinds' feet,
And makes me walk on my high places.

DISCUSSION QUESTIONS

CHAPTER ONE
He's There, Listening to the Cry of Your Heart

Are you ever so burdened with your circumstances that it seems as though God does not care? Do you look at the sin in your nation and wonder, God, where are you?

1. The historical background of the book of Habakkuk is key to understanding the message of this book. When Habakkuk wrote it, what had happened to the nation of Israel?

Discussion Questions

    a.   What had happened to the northern kingdom of Israel? When did the Babylonian captivity of the southern kingdom of Judah take place?

    b.   When was the book of Habakkuk written? What was the situation in the southern kingdom at the time Habakkuk wrote this book? Which other prophet also prophesied during the time of Habakkuk?

    c.   According to the chart on page 19 regarding Jeremiah and his contemporary prophets, when did Habakkuk live. . . during the reign of which king? What kind of king was he? How was he described? What amazing event took place during his reign (2 Kings 22)?

    d.   When the Book of the law was read in the presence of the king, what was the king's response? What did Josiah know to be true about the Kingdom of Judah (2 Kings 22)?

    e.   When Josiah sent to inquire of the Lord from Huldah the prophetess, what message did he receive from God about the people of Judah and himself (2 Kings 22)?

    f.   When Josiah read the Book of the law to the people, what was their response? What kind of things were the people of Judah involved in? What did Josiah do to stop these things? What did Josiah do to restore the land of Judah (2 Kings 23)?

    g.   What was God's response to the people (2 Kings 23)?

2.   The book of Habakkuk records a dialogue between Habakkuk and God. How does chapter one begin? Who is speaking?

    a.   What was Habakkuk's burden? What were Habakkuk's questions to God? What was the problem that caused Habakkuk to cry to God? (Remember the times in which Habakkuk lived.)

b. What was God's answer to Habakkuk? What did God say that He was doing?

c. How did God describe the Chaldeans? What did God say about the Chaldeans' responsibility for their sin?

d. How did Habakkuk respond to God? Where was his focus? What did Habakkuk say to us about the Lord's character?

e. What questions did Habakkuk still have? Why do you think he asked these questions?

3. In chapter two, the dialogue between Habakkuk and God continues. What did Habakkuk say he would do?

a. What was God's answer? What did He command Habakkuk to do?

b. Who are the proud ones? What was the first woe that would come upon the proud one? What is God's judgment going to be on them?

c. What was the second woe? What did He say that they have done? What does He say will happen?

d. What was the third woe? What did God say would happen one day?

e. What was the fourth woe that God pronounced? What will happen to the proud one?

f. What was the fifth woe? What contrast does God give?

4. In the third chapter Habakkuk prayed. How did he begin? What did this show about Habakkuk?

a. What was Habakkuk's plea to God?

    b. How did he describe God? What did God do to the nations? What did He do for His people? When do you think these events take place?

    c. How did the book of Habakkuk end? Had Habakkuk's circumstances changed from the beginning of the book to the end? What *had* changed?

5. What is the danger that God's people face today?

    a. What are Paul's concerns for the Colossians in chapter 2? What do the Colossians and all believers have in Jesus?

    b. What happens when the Word of God is left out of the Church? What happens when you do not spend time in the Word of God?

    c. What place, priority, and pre-eminence does the Word of God have in your life?

CHAPTER TWO
He's There, Admit Your Sin and Embrace Him

Review

Last week you learned that in 622 B.C., during the reign of Josiah, the Book of the law was found in the house of the Lord. After hearing the words of the Book of the law, Josiah humbled himself before the Lord and made a covenant to keep His statutes.

When Josiah read the Book of the law to the people of Judah they entered into a covenant before the Lord with Josiah to keep the law. However, based on Habakkuk's description of them in his book, written between 621 and 609 B.C., there seemed to have been no change in the way they lived.

What is true repentance? What does it mean to trust God in hard situations?

1. Second Corinthians 7:8-11 talks about two kinds of sorrow. What are they? Josiah parallels one kind of sorrow and the people of Judah parallel the other (2 Kings 22-23). Which kind of sorrow is descriptive of Josiah?

   a. What are the marks of godly sorrow?

   b. How did you see some of these characteristics lived out in Josiah? What did he do?

   c. What is the message for you? How can you tell the difference between godly sorrow and worldly sorrow?

2. What kind of sorrow for sin did the people of Judah have?

   a. Because the Book of the law had been lost, what was the condition of the people of Judah when Habakkuk was writing? According to

Jeremiah 2:13, what had the people done? What two evils had they committed?

b. What did God ask the people in Jeremiah 2:18-19? What is Egypt a picture of? What is water sometimes a picture of?

c. In the Old Testament, God constantly shows He alone is to be your source, your sufficiency. How is that same picture seen in the New Testament in John 7:37-38?

d. What had the people of Judah done, according to Jeremiah 3:6-14? What had God told them to do when He redeemed His people from Egypt (Exodus 20:5-6)?

e. According to Jeremiah 3:6-14, what is significant about the fact that Judah had turned away from God to serve idols? How did God describe Israel? How did He describe Judah?

f. What did God allow Assyria to do to Israel as a result of their idolatry? What effect did all this have on Judah (Jeremiah 3:6-14)?

g. Because Judah did not heed the warning, what did God tell Jeremiah to proclaim to Israel (Jeremiah 3:6-14)?

3. What did you learn about the people of Judah in Jeremiah 7:1-28? What did God say would happen if they were to repent?

a. Did they obey? What did God tell Jeremiah to do? What reason did God give Jeremiah for the people serving these idols?

b. Because of their refusal to repent, what did God say He would do to the temple? What did God say would happen to the people of Judah? Had they been given time to repent?

c. What did God tell Jeremiah that the people's response would be? What would the result be?

4. What is idolatry? How could you be involved in idolatry today?

5. How did the book of Habakkuk begin? What was Habakkuk's cry? What problem caused Habakkuk to cry to God?

    a. What did God tell Habakkuk that He was doing?

    b. How did the book of Habakkuk end? What did Habakkuk know he had to do?

    c. What does the name *Habakkuk* mean? What did Habakkuk do?

6. What does this say to you in your circumstances?

    a. Is there a need for godly sorrow over sin in your life? Do you feel that you can't go on?

    b. Are you angry because you are not in control? Do you need to trust God?

CHAPTER THREE
He's There, He Hasn't Left His Sovereign Throne

Review

Last week you learned that there are two kinds of sorrow . . . a godly sorrow that produces repentance, and a sorrow of the world that produces death. The godly sorrow was exemplified in the repentance of Josiah, and the sorrow of the world in the "repentance" of the nation of Judah.

You also looked briefly at the example of Habakkuk trusting God in a hard situation.

Who is in charge of this universe? If God is sovereign, does man have any responsibility, or does man just have to say, Whatever will be, will be? Can these two subjects be reconciled?

1. It is possible to learn truths from Habakkuk's life concerning God's sovereign rule and man's responsibility. How does the book of Habakkuk begin?

   a. What was Habakkuk's burden? What was God's answer to Habakkuk? What did God say He was doing that shows He is in control of history?

   b. Did the Chaldeans have a responsibility for their sin (Habakkuk 1:11)? How does this parallel Matthew 18:7? How is this illustrated in Jesus' words when He stood before Pilate (John 19:10-11)? How do these references explain that although God is sovereign, man is still responsible?

   c. When Joseph had the power to imprison his brothers for selling him into slavery, what did he say (Genesis 50:20)?

d. When God was going to judge the northern kingdom of Israel by allowing Assyria to invade them and take them captive in judgment of their sin, what did God say in Isaiah 14:24-27 about His plans and His purposes? What does this teach about God's sovereign rule?

2. How did the book of Habakkuk end? What did Habakkuk say he would do? Even though Habakkuk's circumstances did not change, what was Habakkuk's final response?

   a. When Habakkuk said the "Lord God" is my strength, what was he acknowledging? What are the Hebrew meanings for "Lord" and "God"?

   b. How could Habakkuk respond this way? What does this show that God can do with the trials of your life?

3. When does the book of Daniel begin, in relationship to the book of Habakkuk? Daniel 4 gives the account of how Nebuchadnezzar came to realize that God is in control of history, and begins with Nebuchadnezzar speaking. Who is Nebuchadnezzar?

   a. What, in essence, is Nebuchadnezzar doing in this chapter? How does Nebuchadnezzar describe God in Daniel 4:3? What does this tell you about God being in control of history? What happened to Nebuchadnezzar to bring him to this point?

   b. What was the interpretation of Nebuchadnezzar's dream? What was the interpretation of the message of the angelic watcher? How long was the decree for? Why? What was the significance of the stump?

   c. What did Nebuchadnezzar need to recognize? What was Daniel's plea to Nebuchadnezzar? What does that show about man's responsibility?

d. Did Nebuchadnezzar listen to Daniel and repent? What did Nebuchadnezzar do twelve months later? How speedy was the judgment? What was the judgment?

e. At the end of that period, what did Nebuchadnezzar finally recognize?

f. What was the result in Nebuchadnezzar's life after he recognized that God was the ruler of all mankind? What did he say that God is able to do?

4. This same truth is explained in Luke 22:31-32. When Jesus told Peter that he would deny Him, what did Jesus say? Who does this show that God is sovereign over?

5. God has certain promises concerning trials that can hold you in difficult circumstances. What is God's promise to you in 1 Corinthians 10:13 concerning whatever might come into your life?

a. According to Isaiah 50:10, what are you to do when you can't understand what is happening, when all seems to be darkness, when there seems to be no light?

b. According to Romans 8:28-30, whatever happens in your life, what can you know? Whatever the trial, what is the hope in Romans 8:35-39?

6. What is the value of understanding the sovereignty of God when you can't understand what is going on . . . when you can't understand how God can allow iniquity to exist without immediately intervening?

a. When you grasp the truth that all things are working together for good to conform you to His image, then what are you to do in all of your circumstances, according to 1 Thessalonians 5:18?

b. What, then, are you going to do in the light of all of this? How is it possible to live in hard circumstances?

Discussion Questions

CHAPTER FOUR
He's There, Remember Who He Is

Review

Last week you saw that God is the sovereign ruler of the universe. He is in control of history. You also saw that although God is in control, man is still responsible for his choices and his actions.

What should you do in the difficult situations, tragedies, and calamities in your life? Have you ever been tempted to walk away from your situation, to forget holiness, and pursue happiness?

1. Your pattern for the difficulties in life is Habakkuk. In chapter one, what was Habakkuk's burden? What were Habakkuk's questions? What was God's answer to Habakkuk?

    a. How were the Chaldeans described? Why was it hard for Habakkuk to understand why God was going to use them to punish Judah? Did the Chaldeans have a responsibility for their sin?

    b. When Habakkuk was troubled with things too hard to reconcile, what did he do?

2. Focusing on the attributes of God held Habakkuk and can hold you. What is the first attribute of God that Habakkuk called to mind?

    a. How is God described in Psalm 90:1-2? How is God's dominion explained in 1 Timothy 6:15-16? What upholds you, according to Deuteronomy 33:27?

    b. What will the everlasting God never become, according to Isaiah 40:28? What will He never do, according to Hebrews 13:5?

c. How can knowing and focusing on the fact that God is everlasting hold you?

3. Habakkuk said, "Art Thou not from everlasting, Oh LORD, my God?"

a. What is the Hebrew word for "LORD," and what does it imply?

b. When did God reveal Himself as YHWH? What did God tell Moses to say to the people (Exodus 3:13-15)?

c. Proverbs 18:10 says, "The name of the LORD is a strong tower." What are the righteous to do? What did Habakkuk do?

d. What does the Hebrew word for "God" mean? According to Hebrews 11:3, how did God create the worlds? If God can speak the worlds into existence, what does this show about His power?

e. Why do you exist, according to Revelation 4:11? Can you change the color of your eyes or add to the length of your days (Psalm 139:13-16)?

f. According to Job 12:10, can you keep yourself alive if God decides to take away your breath? What does Hebrews 9:27 teach about your ultimate destiny? What is the basis of that judgment, according to Revelation 20:11-15?

4. When Habakkuk called God holy, what had God just told him would happen to Judah? Why was this going to happen?

a. What is holiness? If God is holy, can He do wrong?

b. If you consider other alternatives rather than obedience to God, what will God have to do to you? According to 1 Peter 4:17, where does judgment begin?

5. Why did Habakkuk know that the people of Judah would not die, even though the Lord would judge them in righteousness?

   a. When Abraham wanted assurance from God that he and his descendants would possess the land of Canaan forever, what did God do (Genesis 15:9-21)?

   b. What did the Old Testament word for *covenant* mean? What did God promise Abraham? When God made the covenant, what did He tell Abraham would happen to his descendants?

   c. What did God do when the sons of Israel cried out to Him because of their bondage in Egypt (Exodus 2:24)? Therefore, when Habakkuk said, "We will not die," what did he know about God and the covenant?

   d. According to Jeremiah 29:10-11, what did God promise them even before the final Babylonian siege of Jerusalem? How did God assure Jeremiah that Israel would not cease as a nation (Jeremiah 31:35-40)?

   e. In Jeremiah 33, what did God promise He would restore? What has happened to Israel today?

   f. How does all that apply to you? What promise did Jesus make the night He was betrayed? If you have entered into the new covenant, does this mean you will never sin again? What are you to do when you sin? Why does God discipline His children?

6. Habakkuk also called God the Rock. How long had God been known as the Rock?

   a. What did you learn about God, the Rock, from the song of Moses in Deuteronomy 32:1-43?

b. What did the apostle Paul say about the Rock in 1 Corinthians 10:4?

7. How did the book of Habakkuk end in 3:17-19?

   a. In 2 Chronicles 20, what was Jehoshaphat's situation? What did he do? After focusing on who God is, what did he pray?

   b. What does this show you are to do in the hard situations of life?

CHAPTER FIVE
He's There, There's a Purpose in It All

Review

Last week you saw that after God told Habakkuk He was going to raise up the Chaldeans to punish Judah, Habakkuk focused on the character of God. God is eternal, self-existent, creator, holy, the Rock. The same thing that held Habakkuk can hold you.

What principles do you need to remember when you are in hard circumstances?

1. What were Habakkuk's questions to God, after God revealed He was raising up the Chaldeans to correct Judah? What was Habakkuk's problem concerning the wicked Chaldeans?

   a. Did God ever tell Habakkuk why He was using the Chaldeans to judge Judah? How does Proverbs 16:4 explain this?

   b. Can you tell God how He is going to judge you?

2. After focusing on the character of God and asking God why the Chaldeans were being used to punish Judah, what did Habakkuk say he would do? What does this show about faith?

   a. When God is silent, does that mean God has abandoned you, that He does not care? What can you know, even in the silence?

   b. Did God reprove Habakkuk for asking questions? What does this indicate about God's attitude concerning Habakkuk's questions?

   c. How did the book of Habakkuk end?

3. Asaph had a similar dilemma in Psalm 73. What was Asaph's problem? How were the wicked described?

What was the result of their prosperity? In their prosperity and wickedness, what did they assume about God?

a. In contrast to the wicked, how had Asaph lived? As he looked at the wicked, what did he conclude?

b. What gave Asaph the proper perspective? What did God say would happen to the wicked?

c. When this Psalm ended, where was Asaph's focus? How does this parallel with Habakkuk? What do you need to do to gain God's perspective?

4. What is the first principle you need to remember that will hold you in times of stress? How is the fact that God is in control of history seen in the circumstances surrounding the prophet Habakkuk?

5. What is the second principle you need to remember that will hold you in times of stress? What had God said to Israel long before the Babylonians ever became a world power (Deuteronomy 28)?

a. What had God promised Israel if they would diligently obey Him (Deuteronomy 28)? What did God say would happen if they were disobedient? What was one of the curses that God said would come upon the nation of Israel if they refused to obey?

b. What did God say to Judah in Jeremiah 5:25-31 that would be the result of their iniquities? Did this happen?

c. Do you think that God still speaks today to nations through droughts, floods, and so on?

6. What is the third principle that you need to consider when you are in hard circumstances? What will God's purpose always accomplish?

    a. According to Isaiah 14:24, 27 what did you learn about God's sovereign rule? What does this tell you if you think that God is not working in your life?

    b. Whatever happens, what can you know about your circumstances, according to Romans 8:37-39?

7. In the light of these three principles, what do you need to remember about the way that God always works?

    a. Why do you need to know that God always works in accordance with His character? If you judge God from man's perspective, what do you fail to look at? What does God say about His ways in Isaiah 55:8-9?

    b. How did God reply to Job in Job 40:7-9? What can you learn from that?

8. Even though Habakkuk focused on the character of God, he still had questions that God allowed him to ask. What did that show about God? According to 2 Timothy 2:13, even if you are faithless, what can you know about God?

    a. What is God's call to His people (1 Peter 1:14-16)? According to 1 Peter 4:17, what does God have to do when you are disobedient?

    b. When God judges His people, what is His purpose? If God did not judge sin but let it go on and on, what would that do?

9. What difference can it make to you in understanding current events if you know that God is in charge of history . . . that He has a purpose for Israel and the Church?

CHAPTER SIX
He's There, Don't Be Ashamed; Proclaim His Word

Review

Last week you looked at the second principle to remember when you are in hard circumstances . . . that all of history pivots on Israel and the Church. You also looked at the third principle that you must remember . . . God has a purpose in what is happening, whether or not you understand.

What does it mean to wait on the Lord? What is your responsibility to others regarding the judgment that is to come?

1. After Habakkuk focused on the character of God, yet still wrestled with questions as to why God was using this wicked nation to judge Judah, what did Habakkuk do?

   a. When God answered, what two things did He tell Habakkuk to do?

   b. When did God say that the vision would be fulfilled? What does this show you about what God says?

2. What does it mean to wait on the Lord? In the account of Mary and Martha in Luke 10:38-42, what did Mary do, and what did Martha do?

   a. How did Jesus answer Martha's accusations? What did Jesus say that Mary had chosen?

   b. What is the message to you today? If you wait on the Lord, what can you know?

3. What message did God send through Jeremiah in Jeremiah 1? When did the word of the Lord come to Jeremiah?

Discussion Questions

    a. What was God's word to Jeremiah? What was God's plan for him? Where and to whom was Jeremiah to go? What did God do for Jeremiah? How did He equip him?

    b. What did God promise Jeremiah? What did God appoint Jeremiah to do? How did God show this to Jeremiah?

    c. Why did God say He was bringing this judgment? What specifically had the people of Judah done?

    d. What did God say to Jeremiah that He was doing concerning His word? What would happen if Jeremiah were dismayed before them?

    e. What kind of response could Jeremiah expect from the people? What could he expect from God? Why would Jeremiah not be overcome?

    f. What would you do if God were to tell you to warn people to flee from His coming judgment? What if they did not want to listen?

4. When did Ezekiel prophesy? Where did God tell Ezekiel that He was sending him? How did God describe the sons of Israel? What had they done (Ezekiel 2:1-3:11, 17-20)?

    a. What did God say they would know, whether they listened or not? What was Ezekiel given to eat? What do you think this meant Ezekiel was supposed to do with the word of God?

    b. How did God say the people would respond to Ezekiel? What was Ezekiel's response to be to them? What did God say that He had done?

    c. What did God tell Ezekiel that He had appointed him to be? What was Ezekiel to do in respect to the wicked? What would happen to Ezekiel and the wicked if Ezekiel did not do as he was told?

d. What would happen if Ezekiel warned the wicked, and the wicked did not turn from their wickedness?

5. According to Romans 15:4, why do you need to study these Old Testament passages?

6. According to 2 Thessalonians 1:6-8, what will His coming be like for those who do not know God and who do not obey the gospel?

a. In the light of the sin and moral decline in our society—pornography, unrighteousness on television, abortion, rampant homosexuality, the AIDS issue—what must you proclaim about God?

b. What did God say about homosexuality in Leviticus 20? When God told Abram in Genesis 18 that He was going to destroy Sodom and Gomorrah because of sin, what was Abram's plea? Were there fifty? What was the end result?

c. When you seek to be guilty of the blood of no man, in what manner are you to go about proclaiming the Word of God (Galatians 5:22-26, 1 Corinthians 13:1-8, 2 Timothy 2:24-26)?

d. What will your hands be like when you stand before the Lord? Are you warning of judgment to come?

CHAPTER SEVEN
He's There, You Can Live by Faith

Review

Last week you learned from the examples of Habakkuk, Mary, Jeremiah, and Ezekiel what it means to wait on the Lord, and what your responsibility is to warn others of the judgment that is to come.

What does it mean to say "the righteous will live by his faith"?

1. After Habakkuk waited for God to answer, what did God say to him that is the key to all of life, and the key to the whole Word of God?

2. Is faith just intellectual assent? What does the Greek word for "faith" mean?

    a. What are the three basic elements involved in true faith or belief?

    b. How is faith defined in Hebrews 11:1? What does the author of Hebrews say in Hebrews 11:6?

    c. In light of these definitions, what does it mean that "the righteous will live by his faith"?

3. According to Romans 10:17, where does faith come from? What do you need to understand about the Bible?

    a. Did Jesus accept the Old Testament as the Word of God? Did He ever contradict the Scriptures or say that the Scriptures were not accurate in all that is in them?

    b. What did Jesus believe about the creation account (Matthew 19:4-6)?

c. What Old Testament event did Jesus compare with the coming of the Son of man (Matthew 24:37-39)? What comparison did Peter make that showed that he accepted the account of the flood (2 Peter 3:1-7)?

d. What was Jesus' response to the scribes and Pharisees in Matthew 12:28-41 when they asked Him for a sign? What does His response show that He believed?

e. What did Jesus teach the disciples on the road to Emmaus (Luke 24:13-27)? What did this show that Jesus believed?

f. According to 2 Peter 1:20-21, where did the Bible come from and how was it written? If you are going to live by faith, what must you do (Deuteronomy 8:3)?

4. "The righteous will live by his faith" is quoted three times in the New Testament. How is it used in Romans 1:17? How is it used in Galatians 3:11?

   a. The third place in the New Testament that Habakkuk 2:4 is quoted is in Hebrews 10:38. In what condition were the people who received the letter to the Hebrews?

   b. According to Titus 3:5, what makes you acceptable to God? Is it your works?

5. How is it possible for someone to be righteous, according to 2 Corinthians 5:21? When Christ hung on the cross, what did God do with your sins?

   a. In practical terms, how do the righteous live by faith? What did you learn in Isaiah 40:27-31?

   b. According to Isaiah 50:10, what are you to do when you have no light?

Discussion Questions

6. In Habakkuk chapter 2, who is contrasted with the righteous man who lives by his faith?

   a. In Jeremiah 17:5-8, what did Jeremiah say about those who are blessed? What will they be like?

   b. What did Jeremiah say about the cursed? What will they be like?

7. Have you been justified by faith? Are you walking by faith?

CHAPTER EIGHT
He's There, Woe to the Proud, the Greedy

Review

Last week you learned what it means to say "the righteous will live by his faith." You learned that faith is a firm conviction that acknowledges what God has revealed, a surrender to that truth, and a conduct that gives evidence of a surrender. You also saw that faith comes by hearing the Word of God.

What are the woes God pronounced against the "proud one"? Do these woes apply only to the Babylonians, or to all who are proud and behave as the Babylonians, trusting in self and idols rather than in God?

1. God said to Habakkuk, "As for the proud one, his soul is not right within him." How is the proud one described? Who are the proud?

2. God said that the peoples and nations captured by Babylon would take up a taunt-song against the Babylonians. What is this taunt-song about? Are these woes just pronounced against the Babylonians?

3. What is the first woe mentioned in Habakkuk 2:6-8? What will happen to those who do this? Will they get away with it?

   a. Why would they become plunder for their creditors? Who would be considered their creditors?

   b. What went along with the looting? What would you say was the Babylonians' motive in looting and conquering other nations?

   c. What is the problem that this woe addresses? What is another word for greed (Exodus 20:17)?

How does Colossians 3:5-7 define greed?

d. What do you usually think of when you hear about idolatry? What exactly is idolatry?

e. What is God's command concerning covetousness? What did God say to King David through Nathan the prophet after David stole Uriah's wife Bathsheba and then took Uriah's life? How does that illustrate greed (2 Samuel 12:1-11)?

f. What attitude should you have toward material things, according to 1 John 2:15-17? What is forbidden in these verses? What two things cannot exist together? Why?

g. What did you learn from the apostle Paul about riches in 1 Timothy 6:7-12, 17-19? What are you to be content with? Is it wrong to have money? What *is* wrong? What are Paul's instructions to the rich?

h. In Matthew 6:19-34, what does God say about laying up treasures and trusting Him? Why? What point is Jesus making when He talks about the eye in this passage? Does it fit with anything else you've read or learned in this lesson? What are Jesus' admonitions in this passage?

i. Have you ever been a victim of another's greed? Is it idolatry if you have time for a second job to acquire more things, but do not have time for God?

4. What is the second woe? To whom will this woe come? Why is this woe pronounced?

a. What is the contrast between Christ's attitude in Philippians 2:3-11 and the proud one's attitude in this woe? What are God's specific instructions to the believer in Philippians 2:3-11?

    b. How did Jesus manifest this attitude with the disciples just before He was betrayed (John 13:4-5)? What did He tell the disciples to do in the light of His washing their feet?

    c. Are there any aspects of your attitude or your relationships with others where you've been more like the Babylonians than you've been like Jesus?

5. What is the problem dealt with in the third woe? What will happen one day?

    a. There is much violence in our nation today. What is happening as a result of the violence on TV? What does Proverbs 23:7 say about a man's thinking? According to Matthew 15:18-19, what comes out of the mouth?

    b. Are violence and bloodshed always the end product of greed? What does God say about anger in Ephesians 4:26-27? What did Jesus say about anger in Matthew 5:22? Even if you are dealing with righteous anger, what is still your responsibility?

    c. What are you to do with bitterness, according to Ephesians 4:31-32?

    d. Whatever your situation, what must be remembered, according to Romans 8:28-29?

    e. According to 2 Peter 3:10-11, what will ultimately happen to whatever men gained? What will happen to those who do not know Christ?

6. What is the fourth woe? What will happen to them? Why will this happen?

7. What is the fifth woe? Why is it pronounced against the proud one? What is the contrast?

Discussion Questions

8. How do these five woes relate to one another? What is the progression of the woes? What is the root? How does all of this apply to you?

CHAPTER NINE
He's There, Woe to the Drunkard

Review

Last week you looked at the woes God pronounced against the Babylonians. These woes apply not only to the Babylonians, but to all who are proud and behave as the Babylonians behaved, trusting in self and idols rather than in God. You dealt primarily with the first three woes and saw that the first woe was against greed, the second against self-exaltation, and the third against violence.

1. What is the fourth woe? What does this show you about the drinking that was described? Does this woe apply only to the Babylonians?

    a. Is this the first time Habakkuk mentioned alcohol in reference to the Babylonians? What did God tell Habakkuk would happen to the Babylonians because of their drinking? Why did He say this would happen?

    b. What do you know from historical and biblical sources about the Babylonians' attitude toward drinking? According to Daniel 5, what were the Babylonians doing the night the empire fell to the Medes and Persians? Who was king? What were the circumstances? As they were drinking, what happened?

    c. When you look at this woe, what things seem to be linked with alcohol?

2. What woes did God pronounce on Israel that related to drinking in Isaiah 5? How does Proverbs 20:1 describe the person who is intoxicated by strong drink?

    a. According to Proverbs 31:4-7, what does strong drink do to you?

Discussion Questions

   b. According to Proverbs 23:29-35, what are the effects of too much drink? When are you not to drink? Why? How does this affect your behavior?

   c. If "wine betrays the haughty man," what should be the Christian's relationship to wine or strong drink? What does Ephesians 5:18 say? What does it mean to be dissipated?

   d. How is drunkenness described in Galatians 5:19-21? What does it mean that those who practice such things shall not inherit the kingdom of God? If drunkenness is your habit of life, what can you be certain of, according to 1 Corinthians 6:9-11? In this same context, what does Paul say about the Christian's relationship to drink and drunkenness?

   e. Rather than escape through alcohol, what can you learn from Paul's example in Philippians 4:11-13?

   f. What does the world call drunkenness? How does that compare with what God says in His Word?

   g. According to John 8:34-36, if a person is enslaved to alcohol, what is God's cure for it?

   h. How should you live, according to Galatians 5:16, if you want to have victory? How, then, is the flesh controlled?

3. You have seen what the Word of God has to say about drunkenness, but is it all right for the Christian to drink wine? Is it forbidden to drink mixed drinks? Does the Bible expressly forbid the drinking of wine? Does the absence of such a command allow you the liberty of drinking wine?

   a. What does Romans 14 say in respect to drinking wine? What two groups of people does

Paul deal with? What is the response that each had to the other?

b. What is Paul's appeal to both groups? Why does he say that they are not to judge the servant of another? How does he reason with them? What is his conclusion? What is Paul's caution about judging your brother?

c. What will happen when you stand before the judgment seat of God? What is the final principle in this passage that you can apply to determine whether to drink wine or not?

4. Based on Ezekiel 9:3-4, what would you say your responsibility is to those who are drunkards? What did God tell the man with the writing case to do?

5. What is the final woe? Why is this woe pronounced on the proud one? What is the contrast given? What kind of idols were being addressed here?

a. Idolatry involves more than worshiping something you make with your hands. What exactly is idolatry? When does idolatry occur?

b. What command did God give against idolatry in the ten commandments? How does idolatry compare with adultery or murder (Exodus 20:3, 5-6)?

6. Is there any relationship between idolatry and turning to alcohol to meet your needs?

7. If you agree with man's intellectual reasoning that the Bible is not the inerrant Word of God, is that idolatry? What did Jesus say to the disciples on the road to Emmaus that showed what He believed about the Scriptures (Luke 24:25, 27)?

8. Why is God against idolatry? Why is there no place for idolatry? Does God have the pre-eminence in your affections?

CHAPTER TEN
He's There, You Can Walk with Hinds' Feet

Review

Last week you looked at the fourth and fifth woes God pronounced on the Babylonians. You saw that those woes apply not only to the Babylonians but to all who live as they did. You also saw that the fourth woe was against drunkenness and the fifth was against idolatry.

1. What is chapter 3 a record of? In 3:1, what is meant by the phrase "a prayer of Habakkuk the prophet, according to Shigionoth"? How does this prayer begin?

   a. What was Habakkuk's plea? When Habakkuk asked God to "revive Thy work in the midst of the years," what was he saying?

   b. What did Habakkuk mean when he prayed, "In wrath remember mercy"?

2. In verses 3-16, when Habakkuk mentions the judgment that is coming, specifically what judgment is he talking about? Is the coming invasion of the Chaldeans to judge Judah the only subject of this prayer?

   a. What did Habakkuk say God's coming would be like in verses 3-4? Are there any similarities to Matthew 24:27?

   b. According to Habakkuk 3:5, what will happen at His coming? What is the parallel in Revelation 6? What is seen in these six seals?

   c. What events are described in Habakkuk 3:6-9? What did the prophet say God was doing? What parallels are there in Zechariah 14:3-5, 8?

d. According to Habakkuk 3:11, what happened to the sun and moon? How does that compare with Matthew 24:29?

e. What does Habakkuk 3:12 say that God does? How does this parallel the one coming like a son of man in Revelation 14:14-20? What does He do? In Revelation 19:15, what similar description do you see?

f. In Habakkuk 3:13-14, what did Habakkuk say God would do to the house of evil? How does the account of the beast and the false prophet in Revelation 19:17-21 parallel "striking the head of the house of the evil"?

3. According to Habakkuk 3:13, the Lord is coming not only for judgment, but also for what? What does it mean that the Lord is coming for the salvation of His people?

a. Does Scripture teach that God is through with the Jews? According to Romans 11:1-2, has God rejected Israel? What happened to Israel, according to Romans 11:7-10, 20? What happened as a result of their unbelief (Romans 11:11)?

b. What metaphor did Paul use to explain what happened to the Gentiles and Jews (Romans 11:17-24)? What will happen to the Jews if they do not continue in their unbelief (Romans 11:23-24)? What is the ultimate future of Israel (Romans 11:25-27)? What is Paul's reminder about the gifts and calling of God (Romans 11:29)?

c. In Jeremiah 23:3-8, what is God's promise concerning Israel? When was Jeremiah prophesying?

d. In Jeremiah 31:35-40, what did God say about the future of His people Israel? What would it take for the nation of Israel to cease? Is there any relationship between the promises in Jeremiah 31:35-40 and Romans 11?

4. What was Habakkuk's final response (Habakkuk 3:16)? What does that show about faith?

    a. Why could Habakkuk wait? What did he know about God (Habakkuk 2:20)?

    b. When Habakkuk said he would wait quietly for the people to come who would invade, what does this show? What did Habakkuk seem to know about his times that is related to Psalm 31:14-15?

5. What was Habakkuk's great statement of faith (Habakkuk 3:17-19)? What does this teach about faith?

    a. Why could he rejoice? What did he say God did for him in his circumstances? What do hind's feet do for you? What does this indicate that Habakkuk finally understood?

    b. How does Habakkuk's final response show the fifth and final principle you need to remember? How does this account of Habakkuk compare with Paul's attitude in Philippians 4? What did Paul say about his circumstances?

    c. Did Habakkuk's circumstances change from the beginning of the book to the end? What *did* change?

6. God contrasts the blessed and the cursed in Jeremiah 17:5-8. What do these verses teach about where your focus needs to be in life if you are going to be able to handle difficult circumstances?

7. What are the five principles that will hold you in difficult circumstances? Where is God when bad things happen?